GERMANY

GERMANY

BY ELEANOR H. AYER

LUCENT BOOKS
P.O. BOX 289011
SAN DIEGO, CA 92198-9011

Library of Congress Cataloging-in-Publication Data

Ayer, Eleanor H.
    Germany / by Eleanor H. Ayer.
        p.   cm. — (Modern nations of the world)
    Includes bibliographical references and index.
    Summary: Examines the land, people, and history of Germany and
discusses its state of affairs and place in the world today.
    ISBN 1-56006-355-6 (alk. paper)
    1. Germany—History—Juvenile literature. [1. Germany.] I. Title.
II. Series.
DD89.A94   1999
943—DC21   98-15471
                                                                                 CIP
                                                                                  AC

Copyright © 1999 by Lucent Books, Inc.
P.O. Box 289011, San Diego, CA 92198-9011
Printed in the U.S.A.

CONTENTS

INTRODUCTION

GERMANY: A LAND OF EXTREMES

Germany, the land that gave the world Johannes Brahms's soothing cradle music "Lullaby and good night" also produced Attila the Hun, one of the cruelest and most feared warriors in history. Brothers Jacob and Wilhelm Grimm, whose fairy tales "Snow White and the Seven Dwarfs," "Hansel and Gretel," and "Rumpelstiltskin" have delighted generations of children worldwide, brought fame to Germany a century before Nazi leader Adolf Hitler disgraced it by ordering the murder of 11 million people in the Holocaust. Since the early Saxons roamed the Baltic Sea coast in the centuries following the birth of Christ, Germany has been home to some of the most creative, as well as barbaric, citizens the world has ever known.

Germans are known to be fun-loving, robust people who love to eat and drink. The beer halls and brass bands of Bavaria, the country's mountainous southern state, gave rise to the rowdy, fun-filled holiday of *Oktoberfest*, now celebrated in communities all around the globe. Wines produced from grapes grown along the Rhine and Moselle Rivers are prized worldwide. German foods such as bratwurst, sauerkraut, and spaetzle have become regular menu items in the restaurants of many countries.

When foreigners "think German" they picture spectacular castles along the Rhine River or in the rugged Bavarian Alps. They envision grandiose cathedrals whose ornate spires pierce the sky over cities like Nuremberg. They imagine the healing powers of the minerals and waters at health spas, in towns whose names generally start with *Bad* ("bath"). The image of robust, rosy-cheeked German girls has them dressed in *Dirndlkleide*, jumperlike dresses with colorfully embroidered tops worn over lacy white blouses. Their counterparts are muscular men and boys in lederhosen, leather shorts. While such traditional clothing is seldom worn today other than at festivals, it contributes to the image of Germany as a land of hearty, hardworking people.

But it is unfair to stereotype. The land and people of Germany are as diverse as German shepherds and dachshunds. The genius of writers like Goethe and Thomas Mann, composers like Beethoven and Bach, and scientists like Einstein and Fahrenheit balance the side of the scale that paints Germans as a war-loving, militaristic people.

Neuschwanstein castle, built by King Ludwig II from 1869 to 1886, stands majestically among the lakes and hills of Bavaria with the Alps in the background.

East German border patrol guards look on from above as a demonstrator hammers at the Berlin Wall on November 11, 1989.

This darker side of the German spirit has been displayed many times through the actions of leaders like Otto von Bismarck, who vowed to use "blood and iron" to unite his country in the late nineteenth century. Accused, with its allies, as being the perpetrator of both World Wars I and II, Germany seemed to uphold the belief of its Prussian general Carl von Clausewitz that war was simply a continuation of politics by other means.

Since the end of World War II, Germany has paid billions of dollars, called reparations, to surviving victims of the death and concentration camps it established under Hitler. Young Germans who were not even alive during the Nazi era have found themselves living under the stigma of the Holocaust and bearing the burden of these reparations. Understandably, many of them want nothing to do with the German image of militarism and war. Instead they are dedicated to building a peaceful nation that will take its place as a world leader during positive, productive times. The dismantling of the Berlin Wall and the unification of Germany after forty years of division are monumental steps in this positive direction.

The Lay of the Fatherland

1

Throughout its history, Germany's position in the center of Europe has given it power and strategic advantages. It is the crossroads between Europe and Asia, the midpoint between southern Europe and the Scandinavian countries. If Germany were a U.S. state, it would rank fourth in area, about the size of Montana. Among the countries of Europe, however, it is only midsized.

The Influence of the Sea

Two major seas, the North and the Baltic, form much of Germany's northern border. Separating the seas is the peninsula of Denmark, a country geographically attached to but totally independent from Germany. The North Sea is part of the Atlantic Ocean, but the Baltic is landlocked, meaning that it is completely surrounded by land and has no outlet to an ocean. In addition to giving northern Germany a milder climate than if it were bordered by land, the seas have influenced the country's economy as well.

On the west side of Denmark, in the North Sea, are many islands that are favorite vacation spots for foreign and German tourists. Among them are the East Frisian Islands of Borkum and Norderney, and the North Frisian Islands. Some of Germany's major rivers—the Elbe, Weser, and Rhine—empty into the North Sea. This great influx of freshwater means that the North Sea is not as salty as the ocean itself.

Although most of Germany's coastal waters are shallow, there are some deepwater ports and shipbuilding areas where the rivers meet the sea. Both Bremerhaven and Bremen, home of the fabled Brementown Musicians, are major ports on the Weser River. Hamburg, the leading port of Europe, is on the Elbe.

Thanks to the seas, fishing is a big industry in northern Germany. Herring, flounder, and cod are caught in large quantities. The Baltic coastline of Germany's northernmost state, Schleswig-Holstein, is highlighted by fjords, long narrow arms of the sea that reach into the land and are bordered

by steep cliffs. To the east, in the state of Mecklenburg-West Pomerania, the sea has carved many bays, and the nearby land is dotted with lakes. For four decades, much of the beautiful Baltic coast was off limits to the Western world, for it belonged to communist East Germany. But since unification, the area has once again begun to bloom as a vacation spot.

A GRAB BAG OF GEOGRAPHY

The seas are only one of the many natural features that make Germany a geographically intriguing country. Roughly rectangular in shape, *Deutschland*, as it is called in German, is about 140 miles (230 kilometers) longer than it is wide. North to south, the country is divided into five geographic regions that cover a variety of landforms, from the seacoast to the high Alps.

Taking up much of northern Germany is the North German Plain. Along the coast the soil is very fertile and good for agriculture. Moving inland, the land is flat, with occasional rolling hills. Because water does not drain well from the flat areas, the soil is wet, marshy, and moorlike. The melting of an ancient glacier that once covered the region created many lakes. This lowland area gradually becomes drier until it reaches the *geest*, a German word that means dry, sandy soil. Much of the *geest* is covered by heath—a wasteland overgrown with shrubs. The *geest*, too, is dotted with lakes, and several large rivers carve through the countryside. Along the southern edge of the North German Plain is a very fertile soil called loess (LO-us). This powdery mixture of sand, silt, and clay blown in by the wind makes this one of Germany's finest agricultural areas, rich with dairy farms.

Heading south from the plain, the altitude increases and the second major geographic area, the Central Upland Range, emerges. This is the geographic dividing line between northern and southern Germany. The Central Uplands contain low mountains and hills covered by forests. At the center of the Uplands are the Ore (*Erzgebirge* in German) and Harz Mountains, the latter straddling the border between former East and West Germany. Slightly south is the Thuringian Forest (*Wald*).

No definite line marks the change from the Central Uplands to the third major geographic area. But along the valley carved by the Rhine River—the country's major north-south waterway—the mountains give way to a terraced landscape.

Here, in the central and southern portions of western Germany, vineyards produce grapes for some of the finest wines in the world.

Most of the southern third of Germany is mountainous, ranging in altitude from one thousand to two thousand meters. These are the Alpine foothills, the fourth major geographic region. The most prominent feature in the foothills is the Swabian-Bavarian highlands, hilly country punctuated with large lakes and broad, gravel plains. Cutting east and west across the states of Württemberg and Bavaria is the Danube, the romantic river that inspired composer Johann Strauss's most famous waltz. The land here is good for dairy farming and the raising of grains, particularly the hops so necessary for the production of world-class German beer.

In the southern extreme of Germany is a thin stretch of Alps, those rugged mountains better known in neighboring Switzerland and Austria. The Bavarian Alps region is defined

The famed Rhine River, a vital commercial waterway that flows through the wine region of western Germany, is the longest river within the country.

The island of Lindau on the German side of Lake Constance, with a view of the Swiss Alps in the background. Lake Constance is Germany's largest lake and is also bordered by Austria and Switzerland.

by Lake Constance in the west and Berchtesgaden in the southeasternmost corner of Germany. This rugged, rock-ribbed land was the location of Adolf Hitler's wartime mountain retreat, the Berghof. Some of the most spectacular scenery in Europe is found in the Bavarian Alps. Here, the fairy tale castles of King Ludwig II are reflected in the crystal blue waters of lakes like Starnberger See. Outdoor enthusiasts from around the world gather at the Garmisch-Partenkirchen resort for skiing, hiking, and other alpine activities.

A LAND OF MODERATE WEATHER

Germany rarely experiences extreme heat or cold. The country's average annual temperature is 48° Fahrenheit (9° Celsius). In January, the coldest month, temperatures range from 22° F (-6° C) to 30° F (-1° C). July is the warmest month, when temperatures average 63° F (17° C) to 68° F (20° C).

THE FIGHT AGAINST POLLUTION

Like many industrialized countries, Germany suffers from pollution. Its greatest problem is air pollution caused by emissions from factories, cars, power-generating stations, and heating fuels. Concern over the problem resulted in the emergence in the 1970s of a new political party, the Greens (*Die Grünen*), which focused on environmental issues.

In addition to damaging human health, pollution has taken a great toll on plant and animal life. The government reported that by 1995, nearly 61 percent of German trees had been slightly or severely damaged by pollution. Only 39 percent were considered healthy. Efforts are now under way to salvage German forests, hopefully with the same success that its rivers have been restored. In the 1960s, the Rhine and Main were considered almost biologically dead. Little wildlife could survive in them. But after a successful thirty-year cleanup effort, several species of fish now live in their waters.

With unification, western Germans inherited massive environmental problems from former East Germany. Its factories, long shackled by repressive communist governments, were outdated and substandard. Its machinery belched dirty gases into the air and dumped pollutants into the waterways at an alarming rate. Poorly designed automobiles lacking emissions control systems pumped poisonous exhaust into the atmosphere. Since unification, the German government has made environmental cleanup a priority in eastern Germany, but this is a long and expensive process.

Germany's generally moderate climate holds true even in the high country. While temperatures in the mountains do get below zero on the Celsius scale, the people of Upper Bavaria are often spared winter's worst blasts by the regular occurrence of the *Föhn*, a warm alpine wind that blows in from the south and keeps the climate tolerable. An exception is the Harz Mountain region in the center of the country, where summers are cool, winds are cold, and snows are deep.

Without generous amounts of precipitation, Germany would not be such an agriculturally rich country. Rainfall averages about twenty inches a year, but the central mountains often receive twice that amount. Precipitation is heaviest in the Bavarian Alps, where seventy-five inches of rain fall year-round.

GERMAN HIGHS AND LOWS

Germany's elevation spans nearly 10,000 feet. Its highest spot is the Zugspitze, a 9,721-foot (2,963-meter) peak in the Bavarian Alps. Its lowest point, along the northern seacoast, is 6.5 feet (1.3 meters) *below* sea level. Most of the country is at neither extreme. The fields, heath, and rolling hills of the Northern Plain average 325 to 650 feet (100 to 200 meters) in altitude. In southern Germany, where the foothills emerge, average elevation increases to between 1,600 and 6,500 feet (500 and 2,000 meters).

Germany's second highest peak is Watzmann, located in the far southeastern finger of the country that reaches into Austria. Rising 8,901 feet (2,713 meters), it is in the range of mountains known as the Berchtesgaden Alps. In southwest Germany, the section that probes into Switzerland, is the country's third highest peak, Feldberg, at 4,898 feet (1,493 meters). Feldberg is located in the Black Forest, a region world-famous for its production of cuckoo clocks.

The snow-capped, rocky Zugspitze, in the Bavarian Alps near the Austrian border, is the highest point in Germany.

Other German "high spots" include the Grosser Arber, rising 4,780 feet (1,456 meters) in the Bavarian Forest on the southern border with the Czech Republic, and Fichtelberg, a 3,983-foot (1,215-meter) peak in the Ore Mountains along the northern Czech border. The highest peak in the Harz Mountains of central Germany is Brocken, at 3,747 feet (1,142 meters).

GERMAN WATERWAYS

A number of the large rivers of Europe rise in or pass through Germany. The Danube, one of the major rivers of the world, rises in the Black Forest and flows east some 1,766 miles (2,842 kilometers). But the Danube is better known in Austria; only a small portion— 426 miles (686 kilometers)—flows inside German borders.

The longest river totally within the country is the Rhine, which traverses 537 miles (865 kilometers) and forms Germany's southwestern border with France. For generations the Rhine has been a symbol of power and strength for Germans and their leaders. In his book *In Europe's Name*, Timothy Ash quotes a 1989 statement by German chancellor Helmut Kohl. The chancellor remarked that "the river of history was flowing towards German unity, [just] as the Rhine . . . flowed down to the sea. You could try to dam the Rhine, but the mighty river would flood its banks and find a way round the dam. So also with German unity."

As Adolf Hitler's Third Reich was close to collapse at the end of World War II, Allied troops pushed eastward toward the Rhine. "The historic crossing of the final natural barrier to the German heartland [was]," says Robert Goralski in the *World War II Almanac*, "[a] major breakthrough" that led to Germany's surrender. Some 140 years earlier, French general Napoleon tried to build his own reich by forming the Confederation of the Rhine, an alliance of all the states of Germany against Austria and Prussia. He began his move with the French annexation of all territory west of the Rhine.

Not only is the river important militarily, in the south it is the wellspring of the tourist industry. Travelers the world over take boat trips on its waters and view the spectacular castles along its shores. Here, too, are the rich vineyards that produce grapes for world-famous white wines. In the north, where the Rhine meets the Ruhr, is the great industrial cen-

THE UNIQUE BLACK FOREST

One of the finest treats of the German kitchen is Black Forest cake, a rich chocolate cake covered with a thick, juicy cherry schnapps sauce and heaping spoons of real whipped cream. The origin of this delectable dessert is the *Schwarzwald* (*Schwarz* = black; *wald* = forest) of southwestern Germany. Sweet, delicious Black Forest ham is also native to the area.

Topographically, much of the Black Forest is dense. In the lower elevations are oak and beech trees. At higher elevations are the fir forests that give the region its name and make Germany a significant producer of lumber. In recent years, however, extensive lumbering and environmental pollution have depleted many of the forests. Despite several laws that have been passed to protect the woodlands, the phenomenon called *Waldsterben*, "death of a forest," continues.

Although this region is often imagined to be a dark, densely overgrown land of woodland goblins, in many places it is just the opposite. Freudenstadt, in the heart of the Black Forest, receives more hours of sunshine than any town in Germany. The healing mineral waters of the Black Forest draw health enthusiasts from around the world. The area is also home to talented craftsmen who hand carve elaborate cuckoo clocks with stags' heads and other native ornamentation. The city of Baden-Baden is a trading center not only for clocks but also for other crafts of the Black Forest—elaborate woodworking, porcelain, blown glass, and mechanical toys.

ter of Germany. A main transportation route across the European continent, the Rhine is commercially perhaps the most important river in the world.

The Elbe, Germany's second longest river, rises in the neighboring Czech Republic and flows northwest 435 miles (700 kilometers) within Germany until it empties into the North Sea. En route it passes through the city of Hamburg, making it the largest port in Europe. The Elbe is connected to the Baltic Sea by the Kiel Canal, a man-made waterway deep enough for oceangoing ships.

The Kiel is short as German canals go—only 61.5 miles (99 kilometers). The longest, the Mittelland Canal, runs 200 miles (321 kilometers) east-west across the northern third of the country. It connects the western Spree River, Germany's

The terraced vineyards and picturesque castles along the Rhine River make it a popular route for tourist boat trips. A natural border to the heart of Germany, the Rhine valley has also been a historically strategic military region.

sixth largest, with the Ems, a northwestern river that empties into the North Sea. This connection provides a major shipping waterway *across* the country, since most of Germany's natural waterways run north-south. To join the waters of the Spree and the Ems, a second canal is needed. That is the Dortmund-Ems, which runs north-south in western Germany for 167 miles (269 kilometers). It connects the Mittelland Canal to the Ems River. Another major German canal, the 95-mile-long (153-kilometer) Main-Danube, runs north-south through the Bavarian city of Nuremberg, connecting the two rivers for which it is named.

Like some of its rivers, Germany's largest lake is not contained wholly within the country. Lake Constance (*Bodensee*), whose German surface area is 118 square miles (305 square kilometers), is located on the country's southern bor-

der and thus shared by Switzerland and Austria. Lake Müritz, north of Berlin, is the country's second largest lake, with a surface area of 42.5 square miles (110.3 square kilometers). But neither Constance nor Müritz are large lakes by world standards. In comparison, America's Great Salt Lake in Utah is 1,800 square miles (4,662 square kilometers). This great variety of topographic features—the seacoast, the Alps, the terraced vineyards of the Rhine, the rolling hills of the North German Plain—combine to make Germany one of the most scenic countries in all of Europe.

2

THE GERMAN *VOLK*

Several countries in Europe have larger land areas than Germany, but only Russia has more people. This means that parts of Germany are quite densely populated. Dividing the 81.8 million *Volk*, or people of Germany, by its land area shows that 585 people live in an average square mile. By comparison, the population density in neighboring France is only 269 people per square mile, and in the United States it is 71.

WHERE DO ALL THESE PEOPLE LIVE?

Two-thirds of the people live in small towns or rural areas, which in general are not densely populated. The North German Plain, the Bavarian Forest and mountain regions, and large parts of Mecklenburg-West Pomerania are some of the most sparsely populated areas. With the exception of Berlin, former East Germany is much more sparsely populated than the West. Here, less than 20 percent of the German people live on one-third of its land area.

Not surprisingly, the more densely populated areas are the cities. A third of all Germans live in cities larger than 100,000 people. Berlin, the capital, is reaching toward a population of 5.5 million.

Nearly 11 million people inhabit the industrial Rhine-Ruhr area of northwestern Germany, which includes such major cities as Cologne (the fourth largest city), Essen, Dortmund, Düsseldorf, and Duisburg. In the north are major population centers (both ports) like Bremen and Hamburg, the second largest city. Germany's third largest city, Munich, is in the state of Bavaria. The fifth largest city, Frankfurt am Main (Frankfurt on the Main River, not Frankfurt on the Oder River, near the Polish border) is a major European air terminal in central Germany. In former East Germany, Leipzig and Dresden are high population centers.

THE GERMAN-SPEAKING PEOPLE

German is the primary language for more than 100 million people around the world—most of them Europeans. The word *deutsch*, which means "German," was first used in the eighth century to define the language spoken in the eastern part of the Main River valley. In addition to *Deutschland*, German is the native tongue in Austria, Liechtenstein, much of Switzerland, northern Italy, and the border areas of Luxembourg, Belgium, and France. German minority groups in the United States, Poland, Romania, and the former Soviet Union also speak it regularly. Unique to Germanic languages is the umlaut, a diacritical mark consisting of two dots over certain vowels that changes the way the letter is pronounced. Vowels with umlauts are best pronounced by making the lips round and tightly pursed.

The standard and most used form of the language is High German, spoken by the majority of the people. In certain rural areas, dialects—variations on the standard language— are spoken. Often a person's native region can be told by the dialect that he or she speaks. These dialects can be very different. A Bavarian, for example, might have difficulty understanding a person from Mecklenburg-West Pomerania if they

An aerial view of the port of Hamburg. Located on the Elbe River about sixty miles from the North Sea, Hamburg is the largest port in Europe and Germany's second largest city.

were both speaking native dialects. High German began with sixteenth-century religious reformer Martin Luther's translation of the Bible into German. Today, one of every ten books published in the world is written in German. More books have been translated into German than into any other language.

THE GERMAN PERSONALITY

In addition to being a nation of readers, Germans are known to be a punctual, organized people. In both business and social affairs, they expect others to be on time for dates and appointments. In contrast to the more carefree, impulsive Italians, Germans are insistent on keeping records and paperwork exact and up-to-date. Nowhere was this trait more aptly (or grimly) demonstrated than in the fastidious lists the Nazis kept of victims to be deported to concentration camps during World War II.

At the end of the war the German people, particularly the women, demonstrated to the world another strong German characteristic: the ability to build order out of chaos. "Rubble women," as they were called, were largely responsible for the cleanup of devastated, bombed-out Germany. Tirelessly they took to the streets, scraping, cleaning, and piling individual bricks from which workers could rebuild their cities.

Germans are sometimes considered by outsiders to be cooler in their personal relationships than people of other nationalities. In fact, some people say that Germans are more fond of animals than they are of people. Although family life and traditions are valued, Germans are not as child-oriented as some societies. During the last thirty years, births have declined. As of today, Germany has one of the lowest birthrates in the world: eleven births for every one thousand residents, compared with sixteen in the United States and thirty in India.

Since the 1960s, a new dimension has been added to the German character—*Gastarbeiter*, or "guest workers." As Germany began to rebound after the war, people were brought in from foreign countries, particularly Turkey, to work in factories and help rebuild the country. Many decided to stay in Germany, and today 9 percent—approximately 7.2 million German residents—are of foreign nationalities. Turks, numbering just over 2 million, make up the largest group.

Turks began immigrating to Germany in the 1960s as Gastarbeiter to help rebuild the economy, and today they make up the country's largest ethnic minority.

Most foreign workers live in western Germany. Although their relations with the native Germans have generally been good, tensions began to erupt in the 1980s when the Germans realized that the *Gastarbeiter* did not intend to go home. During unification, when the fall of communism in East Germany left millions of people unemployed, irritation with the guest workers became particularly strong. "The *Gastarbeiter* must go!" became the cry. "Give the jobs to the Germans!" Understandably the foreign workers who had made Germany their home and raised their children there were resentful, but most stayed. Today some tensions linger, but generally relations between the natives and the *Gastarbeiter* are peaceful.

THE MOLDING OF REGIONAL CHARACTER

Even though 91 percent of the population is native-born German, each region has its own characteristics. Germans living north of the Main River through Frankfurt are quite different from southern Germans. Northerners are generally blond-haired, blue-eyed Protestants, the type prized by Adolf Hitler as "true Aryans." They speak in more of a dialect than do southerners. Southern Germans are more often dark-haired, brown-eyed Roman Catholics. Particularly in

REGIONAL FESTIVALS AND EVENTS

The differences between northern and southern Germans are reflected in the holidays they celebrate. In heavily Roman Catholic southern Germany, *Carnival* takes place in the spring, just before the Christian observance of Lent. Many towns sponsor parades with colorful floats. Revelers dress in bright costumes and masks, crack loud whips, and shoot firecrackers to scare off the lingering spirits of winter. The Feast of Corpus Christi, approximately two months after Easter, is an official holiday in southern Germany. It honors the presence of Christ in the sacrament of Holy Communion. Catholic saints are honored on November 1, All Saints Day, which is celebrated largely in southern Germany. Sometimes called All Hallows Day, its eve is Halloween.

In the more Protestant north, October 31 is the Lutherans' Reformation Day. This date marks the day in 1517 on which the Reformation began that divided the Christian Church into Protestant and Catholic factions. Although observed with feasting by many northern families, it is not an official German holiday.

In the states of Bavaria and Baden-Württemberg, Epiphany, celebrated on January 6, is an official holiday. This feast day commemorates the visit of the Wise Men to the Christ child in Bethlehem. In Bavaria and Saarland, the tiny state on the France/Luxembourg border, August 15 is a state holiday marking the ascent of the Virgin Mary into heaven. Assumption Day is celebrated with feasts and parades.

Bavaria, natives are more apt to wear "traditional" German clothing like lederhosen and *Dirndlkleide*.

Even within these regions, there are noticeable cultural differences. The rather reserved residents of Mecklenburg-West Pomerania are in sharp contrast to Rhinelanders of the west, who are more carefree and fun-loving. In the east, the Saxons are known to be hardworking and savvy in business matters. Swabians of the southwest, from Stuttgart to Bavaria, are considered thrifty. Hamburg is a liberal city. Prussians of the Berlin area are considered militaristic and conservative.

These regional differences are no accident. They date back to the days when wandering tribes roamed the region that is now Germany. The earliest hero was Arminius, a prince of the Cherusci tribe. He was said to have defeated three legions of Romans in the Teutoburg Forest of northwest Germany about the year 9 A.D. Little more is known about that first great victory. For the next several centuries, while the Roman Empire was in decline, various tribes inhabited different sections of modern-day central and eastern Europe, including Germany. Among them were Franks, Saxons, Swabians, and Bavarians, each with its own ruler. From outside the area that is now Germany came three much-feared barbaric tribes— the Visigoths, the Vandals, and the Huns—who staged repeated attacks on the weakened western frontiers of the overextended Roman Empire.

The Germanic tribes fought back against attacks by both the barbarians and the Romans. In 486, Clovis, the Frankish leader who converted his people to Christianity, defeated the last of the Roman governors in the area. The separate tribes now saw that it was to their advantage to unite, and by the sixth century A.D. they had formed three main groups. The Franks controlled large parts of modern-day France and Germany along the Rhine River. East from the Rhine, to an area east of the Elbe River, the Saxons were in control. In what is now southwestern Germany—a region marked by the Rhine, Main, and Danube Rivers—the Alemanni reigned.

After a time, the Saxons, Bavarians, and Alemanni became part of the Frankish Empire. Gradually the tribes abandoned their individual gods and converted to Christianity. In 751, Pépin the Short became king of the Franks. During his reign, population of the area that is now France and Germany increased. Villages were established and more land was cultivated for agriculture.

CHARLEMAGNE AND THE HOLY ROMAN EMPIRE

It was Pépin's son Charlemagne who greatly extended the power and territory of the Franks. Charlemagne (Charles the Great) is believed to have been born in 742 in Aix-la-Chapelle, now Aachen, in northwestern Germany, on the border with Belgium and the Netherlands. One of the prominent heroes of the Dark Ages (the period preceding the Middle Ages), he supported learning by building schools and libraries. Although he could read, Charlemagne could not write. Yet so strongly did he believe in education that he brought students, poets, professors, and other learned men

Charlemagne, shown here presiding over his palace school, ardently supported education. The Frankish king studied grammar, rhetoric, astronomy, and math, and he tried to learn to write.

to Aix-la-Chapelle, the seat of his empire. He also studied religion and strongly supported the Christian movement centered in Rome. Throughout his empire he built churches and encouraged people to attend them.

Charlemagne first became king of the northern Franks in 768, upon the death of his father. His brother, Carloman, ruled the southern Franks. When Carloman died in 771, Charlemagne was left to rule the entire kingdom. Immediately he launched attacks to the north, against the Saxons, and south into future Italy. In the latter campaign, his forces subdued the Lombards, a tribe that had threatened the area around Rome, where the church was headquartered. Coming to the pope's assistance put Charlemagne in his good graces and helped him later in his career.

During Charlemagne's rule, the Frankish Empire reached its peak of power. In 788 he conquered Bavaria, which made him ruler of the vast region from the Elbe River west to the Atlantic Ocean. North to south, his territory extended from Denmark to the Pyrenees Mountains, which today form the border between France and Spain. To make his empire secure, he created neutral zones along the frontiers and chose leaders, called margraves, to be in charge of each.

In 800, after strengthening his relationship with the pope, Charlemagne decided to travel to Rome to help bring order to an increasingly restless region. There, on Christmas Day, Pope Leo III crowned him "Emperor of the Romans," making him the first ruler of the future Holy Roman Empire. The term *Holy Roman Empire*, however, would not be used until 350 years later, when German leader Frederick Barbarossa added *holy* to illustrate the government's close relationship to the church. In reality, the empire was neither holy nor Roman, but it did consist of what later became the major German states in central Europe.

Charlemagne was a great warrior and a just, knowledgeable ruler. He established a single system of government that served as the highest law of the land. But he also permitted

REMNANTS OF THE ROMAN EMPIRE

Many remains of Roman times exist in Germany today. The city of Trier, on the Luxembourg border, is home to the Römische Palastaula (Roman Basilica). Now a church, it was built about 300 A.D. as the throne room for the palace of the emperor Constantine. This is the second largest Roman interior in existence after the Pantheon in Rome. Also in Trier is the Rheinisches Landesmuseum, an archaeological museum containing the largest collection of Roman artifacts in Germany.

The oldest Roman architectural ruins in Trier are those of the Amphitheater, constructed about 100 A.D. and capable of seating twenty thousand people. Visitors can see the Amphitheater's old cellar where the animals were kept in readiness for fights with gladiators. The remains of the third largest public baths in the Roman Empire, the Kaiserthermen, are visible but are now covered with weeds.

Near Bad Homburg, northeast of Frankfurt, is Saalburg Limes, the finest preserved Roman fort in Germany. Built in 120 A.D., it was part of a 342-mile fortification line that housed up to 500 men. Today visitors can see shops, baths, parade grounds, and the catapults used by Roman soldiers.

In Cologne, settled by the Romans in 38 B.C., is the Roman German Museum, constructed around an ancient mosaic that once decorated the floor of a wealthy Roman trader's home. Other artifacts include the tomb of official Lucius Publicus, who died in the first century A.D., and coffins of other prominent Romans.

The ruins of the ancient Roman baths in Trier. Known as the Kaiserthermen, the facility was built in the early fourth century and contained warm and cold baths, saunas, and exercise facilities.

individual communities to form local governments. He helped create parks, public buildings, and other institutions to help the communities, and encouraged citizens to farm the land. He was respected and admired among his contemporaries, becoming nearly a legend. Long after he was dead, minstrels of the Middle Ages continued to sing of Charlemagne's deeds, some of which were invented and others "borrowed" from the heroic acts of other people. Regardless of their truth, Charlemagne was one of the most important leaders of the land that would one day become Germany.

With his death in 814, his empire began to crumble. Squabbling among his three grandsons, who became heirs to his lands, was finally resolved in the Treaty of Verdun, signed in 843. The terms of the treaty laid the groundwork for the division of France and Germany into separate countries, roughly as they are today.

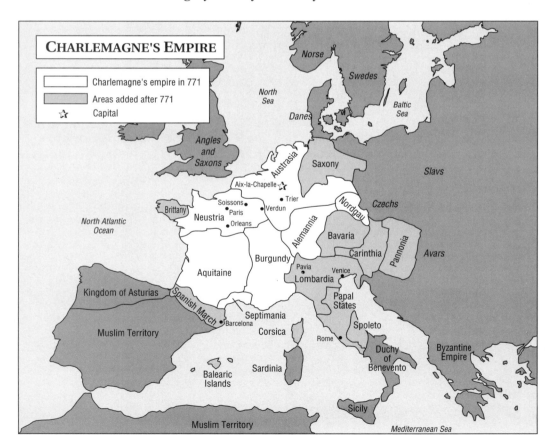

Legend says that some 186 years after Charlemagne's death, German emperor Otto III ordered the excavation of his tomb in Aix-la-Chapelle. Charlemagne's body, complete with a crown on his head, was said to be perched on a throne, one hand holding a sword. What is known for certain is that German leader Frederick Barbarossa removed Charlemagne's remains from Aix-la-Chapelle in 1165 and ordered them preserved in a local church. From this it is clear that early German leaders considered Charlemagne one of the country's founding fathers.

Pope Leo III crowns Charlemagne Roman emperor on Christmas Day in 800. Charlemagne was the first ruler of what would later be called the Holy Roman Empire.

3

THE BEGINNINGS OF *DEUTSCHLAND*

Many historians consider 911 A.D. the official start of German history. In that year the first German king, Conrad I, duke of Franconia, was crowned. Franconia was a duchy, a political unit surrounding the Main River. Conrad's rule also extended to stem duchies such as Bavaria, Saxony, Swabia, and Lorraine. But he showed little tact or leadership in governing these outlying regions.

One year after he came to power, Conrad declared war on Henry, duke of Saxony. Henry's duchy extended from the Rhine to east of the Elbe River. Although they were enemies, Conrad named Henry I to succeed him as king upon his death in 919. Like Conrad, Henry had little power outside the duchies of Saxony and Franconia. He made it known that he considered Germany a group of duchies, not one united nation. Because Henry and Conrad ruled what is today such a small part of Germany, some historians refuse to consider their reigns as the beginning of German history.

THE FIRST REICH

Increasingly, Germany was becoming less of a tribal society. During the next three decades, feudalism established itself as the new way of life. Under the feudal system, a lord granted a parcel of farmland to a vassal (peasant) and his family. In exchange, the vassal promised to fight when his lord needed to go into battle. Free laborers sold their services to the lords in exchange for wages, a sort of early-day capitalist system. Laborers who were not free were called serfs. They worked the land in exchange for food, protection, and a place to live. Serfs were bound to the land and could be sold with it.

Through the feudal period, the future Germany was ruled by Saxons. Shortly after Henry I's death in 936, his son, Otto I (the Great), was elected king. Otto was the greatest of the Saxon rulers. While in power, he suppressed uprisings by vassals and created a stable, prosperous empire with the church at its center. He became a hero when he defeated the Magyars, tribes from the region of present-day Hungary that threatened the German people.

Otto the Great was the first leader to think of Germany as a nation, rather than a group of duchies. In 962 his broad-minded leadership and support of the church were rewarded when he was crowned emperor by the pope. It was the marriage of the once-powerful Roman Empire and the newly powerful German nation. That year marked the beginning of the First German Reich, or "empire," a consolidated nation that would last for nearly 850 years. Under Otto's leadership, boundaries were expanded, culture flourished, and Germany became the dominant empire in Europe.

Otto I (ruled 936–973) led Germany into the period known as the First Reich when the pope crowned him emperor in 962.

YEARS OF UNREST AND GROWTH

It was not easy for leaders of the Roman Empire to be based in Germany. Not only did duty require them to travel to Rome, their domain now extended far beyond German borders, which weakened their power. Lacking strong central leadership, the German princes began to quarrel. Relations between the German emperors and the popes in Rome also became increasingly stormy. From 1024 to 1125 struggles flared, leaving a disorganized government and a substantially weakened reich.

Conflicts continued during the reign of the Hohenstaufen dynasty—a line of successive rulers from the same family. This dynasty was in power almost continuously from 1138 to 1254. The Hohenstaufens took their name from the Staufen Castle, built by a family member in the Swabian Jura Mountains of present-day Baden-Württemberg. During the Hohenstaufen dynasty, the word *holy* was added to the Roman Empire, and it reached its peak of power.

This was a period of growth and expansion. German soldiers conquered new territories. People developed domestic skills and expanded their cultural lives. Advancements in agriculture allowed farmers to cultivate more land. The discovery that horses were quicker than oxen at pulling four-wheeled carts enhanced the trading of produce in central marketplaces.

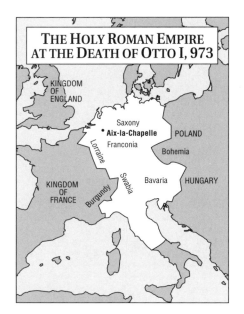

THE HOLY ROMAN EMPIRE
AT THE DEATH OF OTTO I, 973

Gradually people moved together into villages, where the production of craft items flourished. Selling the crafts created a merchant class in Germany. Those wishing to borrow money to go into business often went to the Jews, who were known as the moneylenders, in their communities. Often Jews became the targets of the borrowers' wrath for charging what people considered exorbitant interest rates. Finding themselves shunned from German society in the early eleventh century, Jews began living together in separate parts of the communities called ghettos.

As the economy grew, businessmen began to organize into guilds. These groups were similar to today's labor unions. Two main types of guilds helped protect workers engaged in similar businesses. Craft guilds promoted high quality workmanship and set prices on goods to ensure fair trading. Carpenters, goldsmiths, weavers, and other craftsmen belonged to craft guilds. Members of merchant guilds conducted the trading in a town and sold the products made by the craftsmen. Craftsmen tended to live in southern German communities, while the northern villages catered more to merchants and traders.

THE REIGN OF THE FREDERICKS

Throughout the Middle Ages, which lasted from 476 to 1453, the upper class and aristocrats were often a militaristic lot. Knights, whose job was to protect their lords and ladies, especially enjoyed engaging in battle. They fought valiantly against invaders, and to protect the weak and helpless. In their free time they organized combats called jousts to prove who was the stronger and more worthy of two fighters. As Germany became more civilized, the church frowned on such shows of militarism and the knights had to find a new role that pleased the church. This was the beginning of the Crusades, the religious wars between Christians and Muslims to free sacred places in the Holy Land from Turkish rule. From 1096 to 1291 eight Crusades went from Europe to the Holy Land, supported in part by the aristocrats and upper classes of German society.

One of these aristocrats was Frederick I, also known as Frederick Barbarossa (meaning "Red Beard"), considered the greatest of the Hohenstaufen rulers. After returning from the Crusades, Barbarossa became the king of Germany in 1152. Three years later he became emperor of what he renamed the Holy Roman Empire. Frederick I spent his reign fighting to make Germany the dominant power in Europe. In the process he defeated his major rival, Henry the Lion of Saxony, and Henry's followers, the Guelphs.

Under Frederick's leadership, the reich expanded to include Poland, Hungary, Bohemia, and Burgundy, now part of France. Despite these gains, he was unable to revive the power and influence that earlier Hohenstaufen rulers had enjoyed. A supporter of the Crusades, he died in 1190 leading the Third Crusade to free Jerusalem. Yet throughout his

Jews in the Middle Ages were disliked by their Christian neighbors and mistreated by the government. The medieval Jewish money-lender depicted here was required by law to wear a pointed hat to indicate that he was a Jew.

THE BAROQUE AND GOTHIC ERAS

One of the most spectacular Gothic structures in the world is Germany's Kölner Dom, the Cathedral of Cologne. The Gothic architectural style, popular in northern Europe from the twelfth century to the Renaissance, featured vaulted roofs, spires, and pointed arches that reach skyward, along with endless detailed ornamentation. The cathedral, begun in 1248 to house the gifts the Magi were said to have taken the Christ child in Bethlehem, took more than five hundred years to complete.

Other fine examples of Gothic architecture can be found in the cities of Bamberg, Aachen, Regensburg, and Trier. In the Trier cathedral is the Gothic Domschatzmuseum (Gothic Cathedral Treasures Museum) containing the robe supposedly worn by Christ during his trial. Many castles in Bavaria and along the Rhine incorporate Gothic architecture. King Ludwig II's Neuschwanstein castle was built in the nineteenth century in the Gothic style.

In the city of Coburg is a dark monstrosity called Schloss (castle) Ehrenburg. Built originally in the sixteenth century, it was rebuilt in heavy Gothic lines after a fire destroyed much of it in the early 1800s. The chapel of Schloss Ehrenburg is in the architectural style of a later period called Baroque. Baroque buildings and sculpture retain the rich ornamentation of the Gothic style, but the lines are curving and rippling, rather than harsh and angular. The Dom (cathedral) in Passau is a fine example of Baroque architecture. It is also home to the largest church organ in the world: 17,388 pipes!

The cathedral in Cologne is a breath-taking example of the Gothic style, which focused on soaring height and elaborate detail.

reign, Frederick Barbarossa strongly opposed the pope's authority over the Holy Roman emperor and spent much of his life fighting it.

For some time after his death, a story circulated about Barbarossa. It was said that in a cave in the Thuringian Mountains of eastern Germany, he sat at a table, waiting to serve the reich again when he was called. So long did he wait that his massive red beard grew straight through the table. The call may have come 750 years later during World War II, when Nazi leader Adolf Hitler code-named his campaign to conquer Russia "Operation Barbarossa." Unfortunately for Frederick's good name, both Operation Barbarossa and Adolf Hitler's Third Reich were disastrous for Germany.

Frederick I's grandson Frederick II was a patron of the arts and learning. Born in Italy, he was only three years old when he became king of Sicily, the large island at the toe of the Italian boot. In 1215, at age twenty-one, Frederick II became king of Germany, and just eight years later was crowned Holy Roman emperor.

A likeness of Frederick I from about 1165. Frederick Barbarossa called his realm the Holy Roman Empire, implying a close relationship with the church, yet he continually fought the pope's authority.

Considered, with his grandfather, one of the greatest Hohenstaufen rulers, Frederick II was nevertheless unsuccessful in stopping rebellions by the German princes. By the end of his reign, the princes had gained increasing power in Germany. In 1228, Frederick set out on a Crusade that brought Jerusalem, Bethlehem, and Nazareth under his control and made him king of Jerusalem. Upon his return he launched a campaign against the Lombards, descendants of the Germanic tribes in northern Italy. Like his grandfather, Frederick II had a continually stormy relationship with the church. He finally split with the pope and was excommunicated in 1239, but the conflict continued until his death in 1250.

THE RISE OF THE HABSBURGS

The end of Frederick II's rule marked the beginning of a period of confusion and unrest in German history known as the Great Interregnum (in Latin, "between reigns"). From 1256 to 1273, Germany had no emperor. Nor were there even strong leaders in the individual states. Leadership was scattered among numerous noblemen. Powerful families dominated small territories; chaos, rather than a king, ruled the country. Despite the unrest, Germany's population grew from 8 million in the year 1200 to 14 million a century later. Greatest growth was in the south and west where hundreds of small towns were established.

With the crowning of Rudolf in 1273, the Great Interregnum came to an end. Rudolf was the first of the Habsburg (also spelled Hapsburg) emperors, another powerful dynasty that would rule Germany in the coming years. One of Rudolf's first acts as king was to conquer Austria, where he moved the Habsburgs' headquarters. Increasingly, Austria was becoming aligned with Germany as part of the German Empire.

With the economy growing and trade expanding, the city dwellers of northern Europe entered into an association called the Hanseatic League. The league's purpose was to protect traders and merchants from bands of pirates and robbers who roamed the region. Members promised to uphold each other in the pricing of goods and the exclusion of competitors. The first two cities to join the league were Hamburg, a port to the North Sea, and Lübeck, a Baltic port. By the 1300s, Hanseatic League members controlled trade on both German seas. About ninety members from northern European cities joined the Hanseatic League. For 370 years it remained strong, until the discovery of America realigned European trade routes.

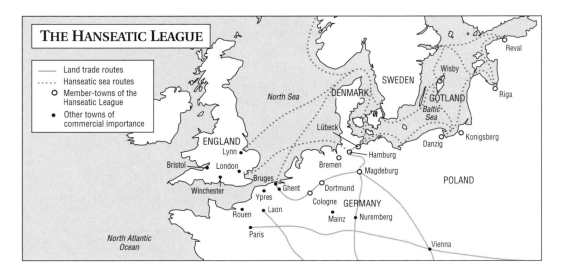

THE HANSEATIC LEAGUE

Land trade routes
Hanseatic sea routes
○ Member-towns of the Hanseatic League
● Other towns of commercial importance

Germany continued to grow rapidly, from 14 million people in 1300 to nearly 16 million in 1500. The growth would have been even greater had it not been for a scourge called the Black Death, an illness carried by rats and fleas. This disease that claimed the lives of 25 million Europeans in the fourteenth century was probably introduced by traders from China. Cities then were so filthy they were said to have more rats than people, and so disease spread easily. The children's story "The Pied Piper of Hamelin" tells of a rat catcher who played the flute so enchantingly that he was able to entice the rats from the city down to the river, where they drowned.

RENAISSANCE AND REFORMATION

The Habsburgs, who had dominated German politics off and on for the last two hundred years, ruled almost continuously until the end of the Holy Roman Empire. But the Habsburgs were not the only major players in medieval German politics. In 1411 the Hohenzollerns, a dynasty known for its loyalty to the Holy Roman emperors, began to gain influence. In that year, Frederick Hohenzollern received from Holy Roman Emperor Sigismund the gift of Brandenburg, the German state that today surrounds Berlin. With the gift, Frederick became an elector, which gave him the power to vote for emperor of the Holy Roman Empire. He also became a margrave, or military governor, of Brandenburg. Berlin, located on the Spree River, became the main residence and capital city of the Hohenzollern family.

In 1440 a Habsburg, Frederick V, took the throne of Germany. Twelve years later he became the Holy Roman emperor Frederick III. Thanks to his children's marriages, Frederick added Spain and the Netherlands to his empire. So closely were Germany and the empire now intertwined that many referred to it as one: the Holy Roman Empire of the German Nation.

This age of the Habsburgs, the Hohenzollerns, and the Hanseatic League was part of a period known as the Renaissance. During the fourteenth to the sixteenth century, Europe experienced a rebirth. This was a time for restoring segments of the culture that had been lost during the fighting and empire building of the Middle Ages. There was a revival of learning and the arts. Music, literature, architecture, and art, along with scientific discovery and invention, once again became important.

German artist Albrecht Dürer was famous for his engravings, woodcuts, and paintings, including this famous 1502 watercolor of a hare.

Some historians say the Renaissance began in the mid–fifteenth century with the inventions of the printing press and movable type by Johannes Gutenberg. Others believe it started with the fall of Constantinople to the Turks in 1453. For eleven centuries, Constantinople had been the capital of the Roman Empire in the east. Its fall substantially weakened the power of the Holy Roman Empire.

While the Renaissance is often associated with Italy, where it reached its first and perhaps greatest height, Germany also made notable contributions. In the field of art, the personable and much-loved Albrecht Dürer brought great changes to Germany. One of Dürer's best-known paintings is the lifelike watercolor of a hare, done in 1502, but he is also famous for his copper engravings and woodcuts. The Holbein family from Augsburg were also talented Renaissance painters. The father, Hans the Elder, was known for his religious paintings. Son Hans the Younger became a famous portrait painter.

One of the major events in Germany during the Renaissance was the Reformation, a religious revolution. For several centuries, problems had been brewing between the leaders and parishioners of the Catholic Church. People were tired of the power wielded by the pope. They sensed corruption within the church: Clergymen lived like nobles, while parishioners scrimped, saved, and denied themselves in order to contribute to the church. Their contributions supported the increasingly decadent lifestyles of the clergy. Particularly vexing to the poorer parishioners was the practice of "buying indulgences." Those who could afford it were absolved of their sins when they made an "indirect" financial contribution to the church.

This practice especially infuriated German scholar and theology professor Martin Luther. In 1517 Luther posted on the door of the Castle Church in Wittenberg a list of ninety-five theses, or propositions, concerning the sale of indulgences. He invited the people to gather, discuss, and debate what the indulgence system was doing to the church. To his surprise, Luther found that many of them not only agreed with him but were ready to revolt against the Catholic Church.

GUTENBERG AND HIS BIBLE

Two of the greatest inventions in history were movable metal type and a press that could print multiple copies of a document. The inventor of both was Johannes Gutenberg, born about 1398 in the city of Mainz, just south of Frankfurt on the Rhine River.

Gutenberg, who was an accomplished metalworker, dreamed of mechanically reproducing the colorfully decorated religious manuscripts. At that time the manuscripts were being laboriously hand copied by diligent monks and scribes. Hand copying made books too expensive for most people to buy. Gutenberg's invention would reduce the cost of printing, enabling the average person to buy books and learn to read.

The experiments leading to the development of the printing press took many years and a great deal of money. Johann Fust, who loaned Gutenberg the most money, finally became discouraged with the experiments and demanded repayment. When Gutenberg could not pay, Fust confiscated his type and presses, including all of Gutenberg's work on a very important printing project: the Bible.

In 1456, Fust and his partner published the Bible in Latin. Fortunately, Gutenberg got the credit. He had designed his type to look just like a handwritten manuscript. Six Gutenberg presses working at once produced 200 copies of the 2-volume, 1,282-page book. Today the few existing copies are practically priceless. Gutenberg died in 1468, broke and nearly blind.

One of the few remaining Gutenberg Bibles on display at the Library of Congress in Washington, D.C.

The revolt was not limited to the indulgences issue. Protesters also demanded a national church for the German people and the right of priests to marry. Immediately Luther was excommunicated by the pope, which did little to slow his resolve or his actions. Four years later Emperor Charles V commanded Luther to appear before the Diet (Parliament) in Worms, a city on the Rhine just south of Frankfurt. There he was asked to recant (take back) his statements and demands concerning the church. When he refused, he was branded a heretic—a believer whose views do not conform with those of the church.

Luther immediately went into hiding. With the help of supporters he created the Augsburg Confession, a statement of twenty-one articles of the emerging Protestant faith. Protestants were those who were protesting against the principles and practices of the Catholic Church. In its points, the Augsburg Confession proclaimed that the Bible, not church

HOLY ROMAN EMPIRE

authorities, was the final word on religious matters. Protestants believed that people could communicate directly with God and Christ; they needed no priests, bishops, or other clergy to speak for them. It was clear that Luther's followers were breaking from the Catholic religion in a move that would never be reversed.

Protestant leaders present the Augsburg Confession, the official statement of Lutheran belief, to Emperor Charles V in Augsburg, Germany, in 1530.

The upheaval intensified until 1547, when Charles V went to war against the princes who were supporting the Protestant goals. Finding his mission fruitless, he passed the reins of German government to his brother, Ferdinand. To settle matters, Ferdinand declared in the 1555 Peace of Augsburg that the princes of individual German states could decide on the religion to be followed in their realm. This resulted in half of Germany's population abandoning the Catholic faith in favor of Protestantism. Southern Germany remained Catholic; the north became Protestant. These divisions are still dominant today.

AN EMPIRE IN DECAY

The half century following the Peace of Augsburg was a quiet one for Germany, but religious unrest was brewing. Allowing the ruler to establish the religion within his state empowered

MARTIN LUTHER: RELIGIOUS LEADER AND ANTI-SEMITE

Martin Luther, who started the great Protestant Reformation, was inspired by a quotation in the biblical book of Romans: "The just shall live by faith." Luther believed that if people had faith in God, God would absolve them of their sins, making the hated practice of buying indulgences unnecessary. It was this revelation that prompted him to protest against the Catholic Church.

As his Protestant movement evolved, Martin Luther developed an overpowering hatred of Jews. He had thought that his Protestant view of the Bible would convince Jews to embrace Christ as their savior. When they did not convert, he was surprised and irritated. His displeasure with them grew until, in 1543, he published a pamphlet titled "On the Jews and Their Lies." In it, reports Paul Johnson in *A History of the Jews*, Luther urged that "their synagogues should be set on fire, and whatever is left should be buried in dirt so that no one may ever be able to see a stone or cinder of it." In addition, Luther called for Jews' homes to be "smashed and destroyed" and the people "put under one roof or in a stable like gypsies, to teach them they are not master in our land." Calling the Jews "poisonous envenomed worms," he recommended seizing their property and ordering them into forced labor. His movement to have Jews removed from the country "for all time" was successful. By 1572, all Jews had been banished from Germany. It was a frightening preview of the attitude and actions that four centuries later would result in the Holocaust.

the princes and weakened the emperor's authority. The Catholic League of Germany, which the emperor supported, was stronger than the Union of Protestant Princes. In Bohemia, now part of the Czech Republic, the Protestants refused to allow a Catholic ruler to take their throne. Instead they recruited a Protestant prince for the position. Outraged at this move, Holy Roman Emperor Ferdinand II of Austria declared war in 1618 on Frederick, the Protestant ruler of Bohemia.

For thirty years the German countryside was ravaged by fighting. From the outset, the Catholics mustered the stronger forces, plundering the Protestant princes at every turn. In 1629 the first, largely ineffective, Peace of Lübeck was signed. As the Bohemians suffered more setbacks, and the execution of many of their noblemen, Protestants from other areas joined the fight and the peace was broken.

The Protestants' greatest help came from a French priest, Cardinal Richelieu. Although the cardinal was Catholic, he greatly feared that Austria and Spain would become powerful enough to overcome France. To protect his country, Richelieu sent money and troops to aid the German Protestants. Still, the Catholics remained strong and another short-lived peace was signed in 1635.

Richelieu now undertook a successful fight on the French border regions that began to turn the tide in favor of the Protestants. The emperor's allies began deserting him, for by now the entire European continent was tired of war and the devastation it was wreaking. At last, in 1648, a permanent treaty, the Peace of Westphalia, was signed, ending the Thirty Years' War. Germany had gained religious freedom, but at a terrible price: The country had been ravaged. Some historians say that the Thirty Years' War claimed a quarter to a third of the German people. It took a full century for the population to rebuild. The economy was equally ravaged. In addition, the emperor found his powers drastically reduced—dealing another blow to the rapidly weakening Holy Roman Empire.

THE SEED OF PRUSSIA

Two important changes in land ownership happened as a result of the war. France captured much of Alsace, a region in far southwestern Germany, which caused great bitterness between the two countries for many years. Of greater importance was the grant of a huge section of land to the elector of Brandenburg, the region around Berlin. Just fifty years later, that grant would become the mighty kingdom of Prussia.

Largely because of the war, the center of European trading moved from Germany to the western countries. For nearly seventy-five years, Germany remained in decay and decline, until the new kingdom of Prussia began to gain strength in the dawn of the eighteenth century.

4

DEUTSCHLAND ÜBER ALLES

The downward spiral of the once prosperous German Empire continued into the first half of the eighteenth century. But throughout these dark years, a small region in northeastern Germany was gaining strength. From the kingdom of Prussia, the land that bordered the Baltic Sea on either side of the Vistula River, the German Empire would rebuild into an even mightier nation than in the past.

THE SECOND REIGN OF THE FREDERICKS

In 1640, Frederick William became elector of Brandenburg. Slowly the Great Elector, as he was called, began building an army. This fighting force helped to ensure Brandenburg's independence and helped Frederick William gain strength in the surrounding region of Prussia. In earlier years, parts of Prussia had been under Polish control. But in 1660, with Frederick William's leadership and strengthened army, Prussia broke away from Poland. To this territory, Frederick William added lands from his other holdings to increase the size of Prussia.

The Great Elector's son, Frederick I, became the first king of Prussia in 1701. Known neither for his sharp intellect nor his physical prowess, Frederick made his mark by spending large sums of money on his court and his army. He was popular with the people because his vast show of wealth made them feel that they lived in a grandiose time and place. His goal, he once said, was to make his court a miniature copy of the French king Louis XIV's lavish Palace of Versailles. As his father had done, Frederick I added landholdings to his kingdom, setting the stage for Prussia to become a powerful and prestigious nation. That day would not come, however, until the reign of Frederick's grandson, Frederick II.

A heathen who harbored no love for his fellow man, Frederick II was nevertheless a great leader and was known as Frederick the Great. He took the throne in 1740, at a time of peace, when the Prussian army numbered eighty thousand men. A year later Frederick took steps to make Prussia a major world power by attacking Austria and later Silesia, territory that is today on the German/Czech/Polish border.

To keep this powerful leader's ambitions under control, Austria, France, Russia, and Sweden formed an alliance that battled Prussia from 1756 to 1763. Frederick financed these wars by taxing the people heavily, which made him unpopular but enhanced his reputation as a great leader. The wars cost him no land and in 1772 he even increased his holdings. Together with Russia and Austria (now his allies), he captured a third of Poland to divide among the three. This was the First Partition of Poland. Twenty-one years later, Prussia was a partner in the Second Partition of Poland. In 1795, during the Third Partition, Poland was wiped from the maps of Europe for the next 123 years.

At the end of Frederick the Great's reign in 1786, the Prussian army numbered about 200,000 men. This fighting force finally met its match twenty years later, during the rule of Frederick William III. In 1806 the emperor of France was Napoleon Bonaparte, one of the greatest military geniuses in history, who intensely disliked Frederick William. At Jena, in what is today the state of Thuringia, Napoleon crushed the Prussian army, causing Frederick William to lose nearly half his kingdom and bringing to an end the First German Reich and the Holy Roman Empire as well.

Frederick II ruled Prussia from 1740 to 1786. During that time, he more than doubled the size of the army and established Prussia as a dominant European power.

It was a devastating blow to the expanding and powerful Prussia, but just seven years later the tide turned. Together with Austria and Russia, Prussia defeated Napoleon in 1813 at the Battle of Leipzig, today a major city in eastern Germany. Two years later, the French general met his greatest and final defeat at the Battle of Waterloo in Belgium. With Napoleon out of the picture, Prussia began to regain the power it had lost in the first years of the nineteenth century.

THE RISE OF THE SECOND REICH

The Congress of Vienna, which met from 1814 to 1815, tried to return order to a chaotic Europe. It established the German Confederation,

made up of thirty-eight states and four independent cities, as well as the kingdoms of Prussia, Austria, Saxony, Bavaria, and Württemberg. Many people now saw hope for a unified German nation rather than a continuation of prince-ruled states. Some even wanted to include Austria in a concept termed "Greater Germany." But unity did not come immediately. The princes knew that such a move would strip them of their power, and they worked against it. There was talk of a "Smaller Germany," one that would not include Austria, but that idea did not take root, either.

Depression, crop failures, and unsuccessful revolutions haunted Germans throughout the 1840s. But in the next decade, the economy rebounded, and the German people felt hopeful again. That hope was strengthened by the rise to power of Otto von Bismarck, a little-known Prussian repre-

sentative to the Diet in Frankfurt. Bismarck's leadership qualities quickly became known, and he was made chancellor of Prussia in 1862. From this position, he launched his plan to unite the German nation by force.

Using the Prussian army to win control of the north German states away from powerful Austria, Bismarck united these states under Prussian rule. His next task was to bring the southern German states into the union. To do this, he provoked the Franco-Prussian War with France in 1870. A war, he correctly calculated, would prompt the southern German states to join Prussia in fighting their common enemy. The following year all the German states except Austria were united as the "German Empire," the beginning of the Second Reich.

Technically the new reich was ruled by Kaiser (Emperor) Wilhelm I. This was the first time a Hohenzollern had ruled the entire German Empire. In reality, Bismarck was its leader. So popular was he at the end of the Franco-Prussian War that he was made a prince and appointed chancellor of the new reich. Many years of European peace followed, due largely to Bismarck's diplomacy and genius in foreign affairs. While in office he created a system of social security, the first anywhere in Europe. It provided workers with insurance against illness, accident, and aging.

Known as the Iron Chancellor, Otto von Bismarck launched the Second German Reich in 1871, an era of military strength, industrialization, and expanded interest in education and the arts.

This period of peace allowed for expansion of international trade. Education and the arts gained prominence, and scholars flocked to Germany to study in its universities and archives. Bismarck poured tremendous time and money into developing natural resources and building up Germany's industrial and military strength—so much effort, in fact, that he became known as the Iron Chancellor. During his rule, the economy of the nation changed largely from farming to industry.

THE WAR TO END ALL WARS

When Wilhelm II became emperor in 1888, Bismarck's power waned. The two men did not agree politically and Wilhelm, seeing Bismarck as a threat, ordered him to resign. Unfortunately

OTTO VON BISMARCK AND THE JUNKERS

In Otto von Bismarck's time, large landowners of eastern Prussia were called Junkers, meaning "squires," or gentlemen of noble birth. Junkers came from moneyed, educated families, but the common people thought them cruel, selfish aristocrats whose goals were power and wealth. This attitude was not unfounded. Junkers considered themselves a superior breed. They talked of a "master race" of pure Germans to which no outsiders, particularly Jews or foreigners, could belong.

For several generations, Junkers held most of the officer ranks in the Prussian army. Being large landowners, they supported agricultural interests. Despite his image as a great leader, Bismarck was one of the most successful Junkers. Historian William Shirer, in his book *The Rise and Fall of the Third Reich*, quotes Bismarck as saying that "the great questions of the day would not be settled by [rules] and votes . . . but by blood and iron." Such an outlook helped establish the image of modern Germany as a ruthless, militaristic nation.

In the years before World War I, Germans were ruled by a constitution that favored the wealthy. The Junkers supported the government and enjoyed considerable power under it. But with the rise of the liberal, disorganized Weimar Republic, they withdrew their support and became almost hostile toward the government. Their lack of support contributed to the fall of the Weimar Republic, which in turn contributed to the rise of Adolf Hitler and the Nazis.

the kaiser's tactlessness in government relations undid much of the good that Bismarck had accomplished. Since boyhood, Kaiser Wilhelm II had cherished the image of the great Prussian warrior. Outwardly he supported his warlike aides and ministers. His buildup of the navy caused much concern among the British, who had long been masters of the seas. And his warlike speeches about the military might of Germany made the world think he was leading his country toward war. In truth the kaiser greatly feared war, but he could not shrink from the image of the iron-clad Prussian leader that he had created for himself. His pursuit of this image caused historians to name Kaiser Wilhelm II the primary perpetrator of World War I.

The war to end all wars began on August 1, 1914. It was sparked by the assassination on June 28 of Archduke Francis Ferdinand, heir to the throne of Austria-Hungary. But the murder was merely an excuse for a massive power struggle that now raged among European nations. Austria-Hungary blamed Serbia, its southern neighbor in present-day Yugoslavia, for the assassination—and demanded an apology. Germany offered Austria-Hungary its support in any action it might take against Serbia. When the Serbian apology finally came it was rejected, and on July 28 the Austro-Hungarian Empire declared war. Russia, Serbia's ally to the east, immediately moved its troops to help. The next day, Germany upheld its promise to Austria-Hungary by preparing to attack Russia, and on August 1 declared war against it.

Within days, much of Europe was involved in the conflagration. Over the next four years, World War I involved 650

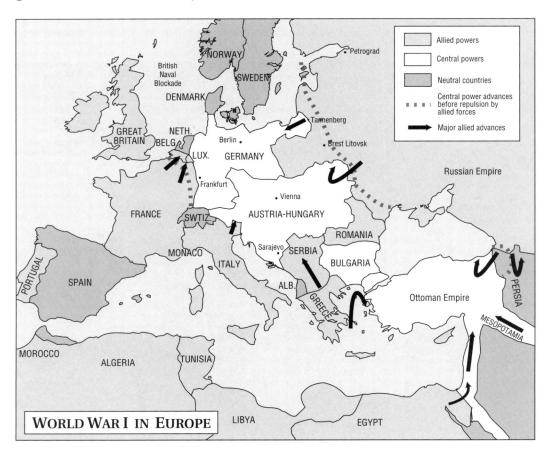

WORLD WAR I IN EUROPE

million fighting men from every inhabited continent. When it ended, on November 11, 1918, 8.5 million people were dead and 21 million wounded. Germany suffered a devastating defeat, and Kaiser Wilhelm II fled the country. It was the end of the German monarchy.

Germany was without a government until February 1919. That month, in the city of Weimar, representatives met to establish a republic—a government that ruled by the vote of citizens and their chosen officials. Because of its birthplace, the new government was called the Weimar Republic. Unfortunately it proved weak and ineffective in dealing with Germany's severe postwar problems. One of those problems was the treaty Germany had been forced to sign at the end of the war.

Drawn up in Versailles, near Paris, France—and so called the Treaty of Versailles—it contained impossibly strict terms. Because the Allies blamed Germany for having started the war, the treaty was harsher on Germans than on the other

A photo taken during the signing of the 1919 peace treaty shows the crowded hall at Versailles. The Versailles treaty, conceived by the Allies after World War I, required Germany to relinquish land, make cash reparations, and keep its armed forces at a minimum.

defeated nations. Germany could not rebuild the army and navy to their original strength. In fact, it could build no military aircraft and maintain no more than six battleships. Huge sums of money, called reparations, were ordered to pay victims of the lands ravaged by Germany during the war. For a country headed toward depression, the order to make cash reparations was a death sentence.

HEADING AGAIN TOWARD WAR

By the Treaty of Versailles, Germany lost much of the land it had gained in the previous century. Poland, Czechoslovakia, and Yugoslavia were reborn out of lands once held by Germany and Austria-Hungary. France reclaimed Alsace-Lorraine in southwestern Germany. This vast loss of land, the restrictions on its armed forces, and its obligation to make payments bred discontent within the war-torn and nearly bankrupt German nation.

Working-class citizens, the bulk of the population, were upset by the weakness of the Weimar Republic. Unemployment was very high. The social security system developed by Bismarck ceased to exist under the new government. Worst of all, inflation was on the rise, making German money virtually worthless. Millions of Germans had lost faith in their government. They were looking for a strong leader who could help them rebuild their own lives and the German nation.

Two thousand of these unhappy Germans were in the audience at the Munich *Hofbräuhaus* (beer hall) on the evening of February 24, 1920, to hear a speech by a little-known but fiery representative of a new political party, the *Deutsche Arbeiter Partei* (DAP), or German Workers' Party. In the enthusiastic, inspiring manner that would become his trademark, Adolf Hitler presented what he called a twenty-five-point program for the party. Each point began with the words, "We demand." The DAP demanded that the hateful Treaty of Versailles be abolished. It demanded the formation of a people's army to replace the regular army. It demanded that the government find ways for every citizen to earn a living and be able to live a decent life.

This was exactly the type of leader that millions of downtrodden Germans were seeking—someone who was attentive to their needs. Adolf Hitler's inflammatory speeches began to resound throughout the country. The party, which

Adolf Hitler's charismatic speeches called for an improved standard of living for the working class. Hitler and his National Socialist German Workers' Party quickly caught the attention and support of many Germans in the 1920s.

he renamed the NSDAP, or National Socialist German Workers' Party—shortened to NAZI for the initials of its German words—gained amazing strength over the next decade. Elections in 1932 showed that 14 million voters supported Hitler and the Nazi Party.

"INTO THE ABYSS"

There was a darker side to Hitler, however, that millions of Germans seemed able to ignore. He hated Jews and various other people he considered *Untermenschen:* subhumans. He blamed Jews not only for his personal failures as a young artist in Austria, but for the upheaval now taking place in Germany. The aim of the government, he said, must be the deliberate removal of the Jews. He proposed that all those who had entered the country after the start of World War I be expelled.

Hitler's obsession with the Jews was of little importance to most Germans. More critical to them was the German government's state of near chaos and the great depression now engulfing the country. The aging and ineffective president, Paul von Hindenburg, had previously refused Hitler's demand to be made chancellor, a position equal in power to that of the president. Now the rough-necked Hitler threatened a military uprising if his demand was not met. Hoping to avoid further chaos, Hindenburg unwillingly agreed, and on January 30, 1933, Adolf Hitler became chancellor of Germany. His appointment marked the beginning of the Third Reich, which Hitler predicted would last a thousand years.

Hindenburg was not the only one who feared that his decision spelled doom for the country. On February 1 Erich Ludendorff, a former high-ranking Nazi who had become disillusioned with Hitler, wrote a letter to Hindenburg. In his book *The Making of Adolf Hitler*, Eugene Davidson quotes Ludendorff's letter:

> By naming Hitler as *Reichschancellor*, you have delivered up our holy Fatherland to one of the greatest [demons] of all time. I solemnly [predict] that this accursed man will plunge our Reich into the abyss and bring our nation into inconceivable misery. Because of what you have done, coming generations will curse you in your grave.

With that letter, Ludendorff proved himself a prophet. Once Hitler was in power, he took immediate steps to make himself a dictator. He outlawed all political parties except the NSDAP. In June 1934, Hitler ordered the killing of his enemies in the Nazi Party, an action known as the Night of the Long Knives. In 1935 he enacted the Nuremberg Laws, which severely restricted the rights of Jews in Germany. Completely defying the rules of the Versailles treaty, Hitler rebuilt the German military into a powerful force. On March 7, 1936, he ordered the army to take over the Rhineland, an area in southwestern Germany that had been occupied by France since the end of World War I.

Finding no resistance in the Rhineland, Hitler invaded Austria two years later, calling it the *Anschluss*, reunification of the Germanic peoples. Following that victory with another, he sent troops into the Sudetenland, the northern part of Czechoslovakia, on October 1, 1938. Still no one made a move to stop him.

In November, Hitler's hatred of the Jews took a violent turn during *Kristallnacht*, the Night of the Broken Glass. On November 9–10, the Nazis burned and looted Jewish homes, businesses, and synagogues, and rounded up twenty thousand Jews for deportation to concentration camps. At last the German people and the world began to look closer at the man they had believed to be Germany's savior.

THE WORLD AGAIN ENFLAMED

Boldly declaring that the Polish army had fired shots into German territory (which was a blatant lie), Hitler ordered German troops to attack Poland at 5:45 A.M. on September 1, 1939. This move ignited World War II. The Germans called it *Blitzkrieg*, "lightning war," a massive surprise attack that stunned the Poles into quick surrender. The effectiveness of *Blitzkrieg* prompted Hitler to try it again and again—in Denmark, Norway, Belgium, Luxembourg, and the Netherlands. Each time he was successful in overtaking the country. By June 1940, France had fallen and German military leaders were setting their sights on Great Britain. Anxious to jump on this bandwagon of success, Japan and Italy signed a three-way pact of support with Germany, thus forging the Axis alliance in September 1940. It seemed that Hitler could not be stopped.

The British were the first to repel the Germans, but they paid a tremendous price: devastation of their country and

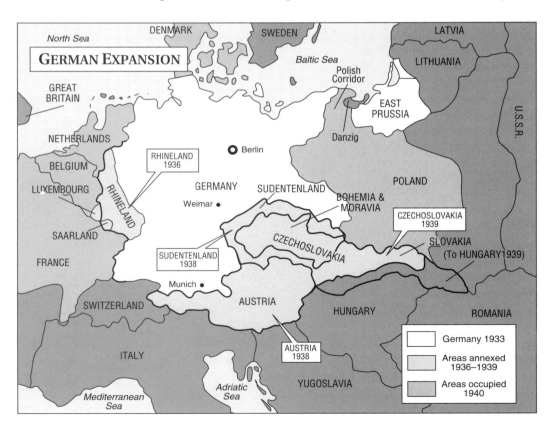

THE HOLOCAUST: THE SHAME OF GERMANY

In his book *Hitler's Willing Executioners,* Daniel Goldhagen writes, "The Holocaust was the most difficult event to understand in all of German history." Goldhagen blames the murder of 6 million Jews in death and concentration camps not only on Adolf Hitler and the Nazis but also on the entire German nation for having allowed the Holocaust to happen. The Germans participated willingly, says Goldhagen, because for centuries they had been deeply anti-Semitic: They hated Jews.

Other historians stop short of blaming the Germans for willingly participating in the Holocaust. They say that the near genocide of European Jews and the deaths of 5 million other innocent people happened because of the Germans' reluctance to help their fellow citizens. Citizens caught giving aid to the "enemy" could be deported to death or concentration camps themselves.

Whether or not the Germans were "willing executioners," they have not been able to escape the fact that the Holocaust took place in their country—in modern, supposedly civilized times. In his book *The Burden of Hitler's Legacy,* former high-ranking Hitler Youth leader Alfons Heck writes:

> The hardest part of my awakening was [admitting] that our regime had indeed committed genocide by slaughtering six million Jews. The obsession to annihilate a race [is even worse than] the murder of five million other "inferiors." The tremendous suffering of our own people, which is often cited as a redeeming [factor], cannot [erase] that burden we bore. . . . While Hitler's legacy may well be my own personal burden, it should remain a lasting warning to the world.

huge loss of life. Having failed to conquer Britain, Hitler invaded Russia in June 1941, a move code-named Operation Barbarossa. Hitler predicted that when Barbarossa was over, the Russian army would be destroyed. For nearly two years the Germans fought Soviet troops who were much better prepared to withstand the brutal Russian winters. As German losses mounted, Hitler forbade his troops to retreat or surrender. But by February 1943, they had no other choice. The defeat in Russia was a tremendous catastrophe for the German nation, and marked the turning point of World War II in Europe. The all-powerful Third Reich, which had once stretched from the Arctic Circle into Africa and from eastern Europe through France, was shrinking rapidly.

Throughout 1944, German soldiers fought hard to accomplish the impossible demands put upon them by their führer, Adolf Hitler. On the homefront, German cities were being devastated in bombing raids by the Allied forces—Britain, France, the United States, and the Soviet Union. Germany's defeat was now in sight, but Hitler could not see it. "Victory will still be ours," he railed incessantly at his troops. He was still predicting victory when Russian troops moving west and British and American forces moving east closed in on Germany in March 1945.

In this squeeze play on the German nation, all that remained was to capture Berlin. With defeat imminent, Hitler retreated to his underground bunker in the capital city. There, he finally married his longtime mistress, Eva Braun. On April 30, seated beside his new wife on a sofa, the führer shot himself to death while Eva swallowed a capsule of poison. One week later, Germany surrendered, bringing to an end the war that had taken the lives of 15 million soldiers around the world and killed more than twice that number of civilians. Once again, the nation that had started this devastating war lay in tatters.

TO THE VICTORS BELONG THE SPOILS

From July 17 to August 2, 1945, Allied leaders from the United States, Britain, and the Soviet Union gathered in Potsdam, near Berlin, to decide Germany's fate. They agreed to divide the country into four zones, one to be occupied by each of the Allies, plus France. The zone that included Berlin was assigned to the Soviets, since they had captured the city. Like the country, it was divided into four sectors.

The Soviets established a communist government in eastern Germany, while the other Allies set up democratic governments in their sectors. At first, relations among the four governing nations were good, but by 1948 they had become so tense that the Soviets cut off all access into Berlin and split from the Allied group. They blockaded the city, making it impossible for food, fuel, or supplies to reach the people. The blockade would, the Soviets hoped, force the Allies to give up control of their sectors in Berlin and pave the way for a communist government throughout the city.

But the Allies did not succumb to the Berlin Blockade. On June 26, 1948, their pilots began an airlift that dropped tons of food, fuel, and supplies to the stranded Berliners. A year later, on May 4, 1949, the Soviets at last lifted the blockade. But the stage had been set for the cold war, a war of angry words, threats, and strained silences between communist and democratic governments that shrouded the world in fear of nuclear war for more than three decades.

Meanwhile, the German people were engaged in the massive process of rebuilding from the war. Those in West Germany, called the Federal Republic of Germany (FRG)—the sectors controlled by the British, French, and Americans—moved their capital to Bonn. They adopted as their constitution the Basic Law, to serve West Germany until unification might happen. The rebuilding process was greatly aided by the Marshall Plan, an American program that provided food, money, and machinery to help the Europeans.

In Soviet-controlled East Germany, called the German Democratic Republic (GDR), no such plan existed. Rebuilding was a slow process that left the East Germans envious of their western neighbors. As discontent mounted, more and more East Germans escaped to the west. By 1961, the number had reached 3.5 million. The communists knew that this human hemorrhage must be stopped. On August 13, workmen began digging trenches, laying barbed wire, and pouring massive amounts of concrete for the twenty-eight-mile-long Berlin Wall. No longer could people pass freely between East and West Germany. The borders were sealed. For twenty-eight

Guards patrol the border between East and West Berlin near the Brandenburg Gate. The communist government in East Germany built barriers around West Berlin to prevent East Germans from entering the city and escaping to the West.

years the hated Berlin Wall stood as the ultimate symbol of the cold war, dividing Germany into two nations.

At last in 1972, the cold war began to thaw. Relations between East and West Germany were established—the governments of the two countries were finally speaking to each other. Soviet leader Mikhail Gorbachev promoted his plans for *perestroika* (reorganization) and *glasnost* (greater open-

THE LONG ROAD TO UNIFICATION

The leader who restored West Germany to a respectable place in the world and contributed to the miracle of German rebirth after World War II was Konrad Adenauer, first chancellor of the FRG. Throughout his term, from 1949 to 1963, he was highly respected, both in foreign and domestic affairs. Adenauer, who had no tolerance for communism, saw no hope for unification as long as East Germany remained communist. He died in 1966, before any prospect of a communist-free, united Germany had been born.

The man who led the country to unification was Helmut Kohl, who became West Germany's chancellor in 1982. Despite the GDR leaders' resistance to unification, by 1989 the East German people could not be stopped. On September 11, sixteen thousand East Germans left the country through a newly opened border between Hungary and Austria. The following month communist party leaders, seeing their control crumbling, pressed general secretary Erich Honecker to resign.

In November, Kohl announced his plan for unification. It was met by a flat "No" from the new leaders of the GDR. But his determination and the spirit of the East German people were stronger. In March 1990, the communist government allowed the first free elections in East Germany in forty-one years. The new leaders favored unification, and West German money began to flow to the struggling and underdeveloped East Germany. On October 3, East and West Germany at last became one.

Helmut Kohl oversaw the reunification of Germany on October 3, 1990.

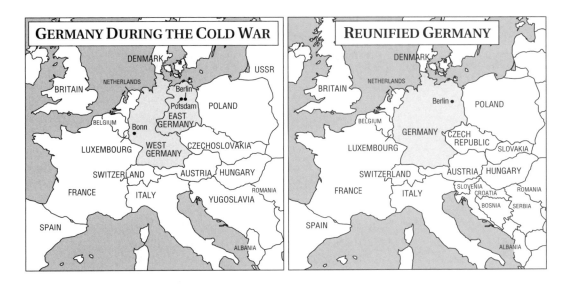

ness). In many communist countries of Europe and Asia, citizens began calling for the removal of repressive leaders. In East Germany that leader was Erich Honecker, in power nearly twenty years. On October 7, 1989, during celebrations marking the fortieth anniversary of East Germany, demonstrations were staged against Honecker. The people demanded his removal from office, and they got it.

One month later on November 9, under increasing pressure from East German citizens and humanitarian groups around the world, the communist government opened the Berlin Wall. Dismantling the wall paved the way for unification one year later. At last, on October 3, 1990, after forty-one years of being divided, Germany became a united nation once again. *Deutschland Über Alles,* "Germany Above All," remains the motto of nationalistic pride that has bonded Germans for generations.

5

GERMANY TODAY

A brochure published by the German government's press department reported in the mid-1990s:

> Unification of Germany is on track, but far from complete. . . . The state of the economy, the environment and the infrastructure in East Germany was far worse than anybody had expected. Telephone systems, the railroads, most industries were hopelessly antiquated, some beyond redemption. Real unification will not be achieved until living conditions . . . are at least similar in both parts of the country. This will take time and money. Lots of it. It will also take a certain amount of tact, never a typical German characteristic. . . . East Germans often complain that Western Germans are condescending and do not appreciate their achievements. West Germans sometimes find East Germans too demanding and impatient. . . . The problem of real integration will [only] be solved by the passage of time.

The united German nation is now called the Federal Republic of Germany. Its government is structured around the Basic Law, the constitution that was developed for West Germany in 1949. "Federal" means that the country is a union of states, called *Länder*, under one central government. A "republic" is a government where the power rests with the people, who vote in free elections for representatives who will carry out their wishes.

Germany's head of state is the president, who is elected by the Federal Assembly—a parliamentary body generally referred to as the *Bundestag*—for a term of five years. The president is concerned primarily with matters of foreign policy. The most powerful official, the one who carries out its domestic affairs, is the chancellor, who serves as head of the executive branch of government. The Federal Assembly is made up of representatives who are elected to the *Bundestag*, the lower house of Parliament, for a term of four years. In the upper house, or *Bundesrat*, representatives are appointed from the sixteen states.

GERMANY AND THE EUROPEAN UNION

Centuries of rivalry and strife among European nations may come to an end in the new century with the emerging European Union (EU). Thus far Germany and fourteen other nations have pledged allegiance to the EU, the new union of European states, and more are expected to join.

The EU's purpose is to bind the nations of Europe under one political and economic umbrella while maintaining the individuality of each country. It promotes a common European identity rather than encouraging rivalrous, nationalistic feelings among European nations.

The European Union has its own form of government. Members now share one flag and celebrate Europe Day on May 9. Soon they will share a common currency, the Euro. In the future, residents of member countries will claim a common European citizenship and vote on EU matters. No longer will there be border checks for people passing from one member country to another.

German officials hope the EU will make Europe competitive in world trading by exporting the goods and services of many countries. They want the buying power of a large nation when they are importing goods. State officials, however, fear that one day the EU may hold more power over the states than does the German government. German manufacturers worry that unskilled or semiskilled jobs may be moved to places in the EU where labor is cheaper. Some bankers and businesspeople fear mingling the strong German deutsche mark with the less stable currencies of other countries.

A meeting of the European Union, a political and economic union of European nations, including Germany.

GETTING AN EDUCATION

The Basic Law provides for a government-supported school system throughout Germany. Today's 52,000 schools are staffed by nearly 750,000 teachers and attended by 12.2 million students. Schooling is free, and children ages six to eighteen must attend. Most books and educational materials are also free. Kindergarten, although a German concept, is not part of the state school system. German kindergartens are operated privately, but all children are assured a place if they wish to attend. Parents pay on a sliding scale, based on their income.

Grundschule, or primary school, begins at age six and generally lasts four years (six in some areas). Most German primary schools do not issue grades. Instead they send reports to parents describing children's strengths and weaknesses. Religion is a required subject for all German children through the age of fourteen.

At age ten, students must choose among three types of schooling they must attend for the next five to six years. *Hauptschule* is an apprenticeship program attended by about 25 percent of students. In *Hauptschule* they study math, science, and reading and also learn skills that will help them in a trade. By age sixteen they are ready for a trade school that will prepare them for careers in construction, food service, health and beauty care, and the like.

German children attend primary school until age ten, then choose a specialized secondary school (Realschule, Hauptschule, *or* Gymnasium) *to continue their education.*

Students who choose *Realschule* after the primary years are preparing for a technical school, which they enter at age sixteen. *Realschule* provides a stronger, more comprehensive education than *Hauptschule*. It teaches business and secretarial skills, computer programming and operation, and generally prepares students for careers in business, industry, or public service. Both *Hauptschule* and *Realschule* offer excellent vocational and apprenticeship training.

Gymnasium prepares students for the university. This college preparatory education lasts through grade twelve in some states, grade thirteen in others. Students must take courses from three major areas: social sciences; math, science, and technology; and literature and the arts, which generally includes two foreign languages. The competition for space at German universities is very tight, so students must be well prepared when they leave *Gymnasium*.

The length of the German school day is often up to the teacher. Most schools start at about 8:00 A.M. and last until noon at the primary level, early afternoon at the secondary level. The school year runs eleven months, with a month's vacation in August and several shorter holidays throughout the year. Some areas hold school on Saturday. In general, German students take school very seriously because the competition to get into college or into a good trade/technical school is intense.

GERMAN YOUTH AND SOCIAL SERVICES

The new Germany is a youthful country. Students and young people under eighteen make up nearly 20 percent of the population. About one in ten of them is foreign-born. A third of all Germans are under twenty-seven years of age. This youthful profile is due partly to the fact that many who would now be Germany's senior citizens were killed during the war years or suffered early deaths from war-related causes. In the 1940s and '50s, birthrates were low because of the hard times Germans were enduring in rebuilding their nation.

Today's young Germans (95 percent in the west and 84 percent in the east) say they are satisfied with life. They feel their chances for achieving a reasonable standard of living are good. As in other Western nations, young Germans do not depend as much on traditions, religion, or family ties as they did in the past. They follow the moral lead of their

Soccer is one of the most popular sports in Germany. Young Germans enjoy watching professional soccer games and playing soccer themselves in sports clubs.

peers rather than that of adults, and are influenced by fads and the media in our increasingly global world.

Clubs and organizations—of which there are nearly 300,000 in the country—are popular with German youth, particularly in the west. Young people patronize sports clubs, religious and political organizations, and community groups that attend concerts, go to movies and museums, and party in trendy nightclubs. There are clubs for nearly every type of interest or hobby, from dog breeding to stamp collecting. Although families are responsible for their children's leisure time activities, the government spends a considerable amount of money under the Federal Child and Youth Plan to help finance these organizations.

With few exceptions, Germany has had excellent social security programs since the days of Bismarck. In addition to its support of children and youth, the government offers other types of social security benefits. The Basic Law says that the government must provide assistance in health and accident insurance, old age pensions, housing, and unemployment benefits. Aid to the poor ensures that every citizen will have at least a minimal standard of living. Although these benefits are "free," citizens are taxed heavily to support such extensive social programs. A third of Germany's gross national product (GNP), the value of goods and services it produces in a year, is spent on social security benefits.

EARNING A LIVING

After the fall of the East German government in 1989–1990, unemployment in the former communist states soared. Under communism, all citizens had jobs, but many were nonessential. They were created only to ensure full employment. When communism died, East Germans found many of their nonessential jobs died with it. Those who did hold necessary positions discovered that their job skills were lacking compared with their better-trained and more experienced West German counterparts. Since unification, the government has provided additional training, equipment, and job opportunities for millions of eastern Germans, so the situation is slowly improving.

The unified Germany now has about 2.5 million unemployed workers in a labor force of nearly 40 million people. Approximately 40 percent of the employed people work in industry, many in manufacturing. Factories produce cars and ships, electrical equipment, optical products, and machine tools. Other industries produce iron, steel, and chemicals. For generations, the Ruhr district of North Rhine-Westphalia has been Germany's center of heavy industry, where coal and steel are produced. The centers for auto production are in Bavaria and Baden-Württemberg, the latter also being a large chemical production region. In eastern Germany, Saxon-Anhalt and Thuringia are the major manufacturing areas.

Many of Germany's major industrial companies are known worldwide. Daimler-Benz and Volkswagen are big names in auto manufacturing. The giant chemical company Bayer is best known for its aspirin, and Siemens, for precision electronic devices. Although they employ hundreds of thousands of people, these big companies do not provide a majority of the industrial jobs. Most German industrial workers—98 percent—work for small or midsized companies that employ five hundred or fewer people.

Crafters and tradesmen make up a large segment of these smaller companies. Crafts have been an important part of the economy since the medieval trade guilds. Today some 6.2 million German craftsmen create products like hand-crafted

GERMANY'S INDUSTRIAL GIANTS*

1. **Daimler-Benz:** Germany's largest company in terms of annual sales, approximately $73 billion. Makers of Mercedes Benz cars, other automotive products, and aerospace equipment. Headquartered in Stuttgart, the company employs approximately 331,000 people.
2. **Siemens:** Largest manufacturer of electronic equipment in Germany, employing 382,000 people, with headquarters in Munich. Annual sales about $60 billion.
3. **Volkswagen:** Automaker located in Wolfsburg, employs nearly a quarter-million people and has yearly sales of $56 billion.
4. **VEBA:** The largest energy and chemical company in Germany, centered in Düsseldorf. Employs 127,000 workers with sales of $45.5 billion per year.
5. **Hoechst:** Giant pharmaceutical and chemical company in Frankfurt am Main, has approximately 166,000 employees and does annual sales of $35 billion.
6. **RWE:** An energy and construction giant located in Essen, employs 119,000 people; sales of just over $32 billion per year.
7. **BASF:** Chemical and pharmaceutical company headquartered in Ludwigshafen has just over 100,000 employees—though fewer than its close rival, Bayer, its annual sales are greater: nearly $33 billion. BASF, Bayer, and Hoechst have controlled Germany's pharmaceutical industry for more than a century.
8. **Bayer:** Located in Leverkusen, pharmaceutical and chemical company best known for its aspirin; employs 147,000 people and does annual sales of nearly $31 billion per year.
9. **Bayerische Motorenwerke:** Manufacturers of BMW and other automotive products, this Munich-based company employs nearly 110,000 people and does nearly $30 billion a year in sales.
10. **Thyssen:** A steel and machinery manufacturer in Duisburg, has a workforce of nearly 132,000 and does approximately $25 billion a year in sales.
11. **Bosch:** Internationally known manufacturer of electrical products; based in Stuttgart, employs approximately 156,000 people. Annual sales are approximately $24 billion.

*Ranked in order of annual sales

Car production at the Daimler-Benz factory in Stuttgart. Daimler-Benz is Germany's highest-grossing company.

cuckoo clocks and fine pastries, or engage in trades like carpentry and plumbing. To ensure high-quality work among craftsmen and tradespeople, the federal court has ruled that business owners must have a master's status in their fields.

Agriculture, once the backbone of the German economy, now supports only a small number of workers. In 1950, there were 1.6 million farms; today there are just over half a million. About 275,000 people—mostly family members—work these farms. Improved methods have made production much more efficient, so more crops are produced per employee than in the past. The vineyards that grow grapes for famous German wines are part of the agriculture along the Rhine River and in certain other parts of the country. Fishing and forestry are also considered "agricultural" pursuits. Together they contribute 1.1 percent of Germany's annual GNP.

HOW GERMANS SPEND THEIR LEISURE TIME

German workers enjoy more hours of free time than workers anywhere in the industrial world. The average German spends 1,708 hours at work each year, compared with 1,912 hours for American workers and 2,166 for Japanese workers. German efficiency is due in part to the country's excellent system of trade and technical schools. Students graduate with an in-depth knowledge of their fields and the skills necessary to perform well in the workplace.

How do Germans spend their average six weeks of vacation time each year? Travel is extremely popular. More than half of all Germans spend at least five vacation days away from home. East Germans are particularly enthusiastic travelers, since for many years they were restricted to their own

PROMINENT GERMAN ATHLETES

Steffi Graf, tennis: Seven-time winner of the women's singles title at the Wimbledon competition in England. Born in West Germany in 1969, became an Olympic champion in 1984; three years later declared best female tennis player in the world.

Boris Becker, tennis: At seventeen, youngest person to win the men's singles at Wimbledon. West German–born athlete also carried his team to two Davis Cup championships.

Kornelia Ender and Kirstin Otto, swimming: Both born in East Germany, won a total of thirteen Olympic medals for their country. Ender won three silver medals in the 1972 Summer Olympics and four gold in 1976. Otto took six gold in 1988.

Roland Matthes, swimming: West German set sixteen world records from 1967 to 1973, and won gold at the 1968 and 1972 Olympics.

Katarina Witt, figure skating: Born in East Germany in 1965, took gold medals in the 1984 and 1988 Olympic Games; four-time world champion during those years.

Rosi Mittermeier, alpine skiing: West German won Olympic gold in downhill and slalom during the 1976 Winter Olympics.

Jens Weissflog, skiing: Most successful German ski jumper of all time, won the 120-meter Nordic jumping event at the 1994 Olympics.

Germany's national soccer team has won the World Cup three times. **Franz Beckenbauer** captained the championship team in 1974 and coached the team to victory in 1990.

Steffi Graf is one of Germany's most well known tennis champions.

country. The most popular foreign destinations are southern Europe and the United States. Within Germany, the islands of the North Sea are a popular vacation spot, as are the Bavarian Alps.

Sports are one of the most popular leisure time activities. Not only do Germans enjoy watching soccer, tennis, gymnastics, skating, skiing, and other professional events, they are also active participants. Some 26 million Germans belong to more than eighty-five thousand sports clubs, and another 12 million pursue their favorite sports on an individual basis. The largest sports organization in the country is the *Deutscher Fussball* (Soccer) *Bund*. The German Sports Federation is a countrywide organization with sixteen regional divisions that coordinate facilities, coaching, and competitive events for amateur sportspeople.

Most Germans participate in sports not to become professional athletes but because they enjoy exercising and keeping their bodies in shape. This national health consciousness prompts Germans to spend time at spas, soaking in the hot springs and drinking the healing mineral water. At home, they patronize more than fifty-five hundred fitness centers around the country.

German people are enthusiastic museum goers, and with good reason—the country has more than three thousand of them. Visitors can find collections ranging from exquisite Easter eggs to the world's largest cuckoo clock (at Schonach in the Black Forest). Equipment for wine making and drinking can be seen at the Rheingau Wine Museum in Rüdesheim. The Bundespost Museum in Frankfurt houses collections of stamps, telephones, radios, and even buses. This is only a small sample of the types of attractions that can be found in Germany's museums.

ENJOYING THE ARTS

Germans spend far less leisure time watching television than do Americans. The average German watches only about two hours a day, less than half the daily average of American viewers. In Germany there are eleven regional broadcasting companies, both TV and radio, and one national network prescribed by the Basic Law. A second network operates under an agreement between the individual states and the broadcasting company. Germans trust the electronic media,

The audience sits on all sides of the orchestra at a performance of the world-renowned Berlin Philharmonic. Germany is a nation of avid music lovers and supports the arts through private and government funds.

as shown in a recent survey where 51 percent ranked television over all other media as their primary source for political news.

Television has stolen much of the audience from the once highly rated German film industry. In the 1950s, more than a billion people a year attended the cinema, compared with only 125 million in 1995. Another factor affecting German film production is the overwhelming popularity of the Hollywood blockbusters. Despite talented native filmmakers, German-made films now draw only 10 percent of total audiences.

Music and live theater are very popular in Germany. The country's rich musical heritage is alive today in its 121 opera houses, the oldest of which is the one built in Hamburg in 1678. Among Germany's 141 professional orchestras, the best known is the Berlin Philharmonic, one of the finest in the world. Supporting Germans' love of plays and acting are 160 public and 190 private theaters. On the modern scene, musicians like the rock group Die Prinzen and the pop group Pur perform in concerts worldwide. Music and drama are supported in part by government money to ensure their continuation and high quality. Each year, 35 million people attend 100,000 theater performances and concerts, which would not be possible without support from public funds.

Likewise, government and private aid are available for the visual arts, to help struggling artists support themselves in a field where it is difficult to earn a secure living. Germans have long been highly appreciative of art, and the country is alive with art museums and galleries. Many specialize in the modern, abstract works of contemporary painters. The National Gallery in Berlin has an excellent collection by world-renowned portrait artist Max Liebermann. Electronic art forms have become popular in recent years, combining human talent with the latest advances in technology. Two centers for this new medium are the Städel Art Institute in Frankfurt and the Center for Art and Media in Karlsruhe.

Since the eleventh century, when wandering minstrels first performed at court, Germany has been a highly literate nation. Today the country ranks second after the United States in number of books produced—nearly seventy thousand new titles per year. Annually in October, Frankfurt hosts the world's largest book fair, drawing publishers, authors, booksellers, and thousands of readers from around the world. Another major international book fair is held in Leipzig each spring. These fairs give Germans a well-deserved reputation as a nation of book lovers who ranks reading and the arts among its favorite leisure time activities.

6 HISTORY LIVES ON

Germany's thousand years of history are remembered today in its museums, architecture, and countless festivals. The country's polycentrist development—its growth in many regions rather than one central area—is reflected in the differences in architecture and folk festivals from one part of *Deutschland* to another. The newest national holiday is German Unity Day, October 3. The anniversary of unification is marked by the closing of state and federal offices and most businesses.

RELIGIOUS HOLIDAYS

Germany, a land long associated with the printing of beautiful Christmas cards, has many traditions woven into its celebration of *Weihnachten*. On December 6, Germans celebrate the Feast of St. Nicholas. On that day, the gift-giving saint arrives to hide nuts and candy in good children's shoes or stockings. Those who have not been good are visited by the frightening, black-robed Ruprecht, who wields a big stick.

On December 24, families repeat a worldwide Christian tradition that began in Germany: decorating the *Tannenbaum*. After the tree is decorated, parents ring a tiny silver bell signaling that children may open their gifts. Families then gather for a festive meal, traditionally goose, although many people now eat turkey. Dessert may include *Lebkuchen*, a spicy Bavarian gingerbread, or stollen, a breadlike cake made with nuts and dried fruit. At midnight the faithful go to church to culminate the season celebrating Christ's birth. Epiphany on January 6, the day Christians believe the three Wise Men visited the newborn Christ child, marks the end of the Christmas season.

Fasching, another Christian celebration, is celebrated largely in Bavaria, but also in the regions around Cologne, Mainz, Bonn, Düsseldorf, Offenburg, and the Black Forest. This is a time of merrymaking that precedes Lent, the period of fasting and penance in preparation for Easter. *Fasching* occurs during January and February with carnivals, parades, and street fairs similar to those at Mardi Gras. There are masked balls, carnival princes are crowned, and on the last Tuesday of the season—Shrove ("Fat") Tuesday—people feast in preparation for the upcoming fast.

Easter, in March or April, is another multiday observance, celebrated differently throughout the country. Good Friday, two days before Easter Sunday, is remembered solemnly by Christians as the day Christ was crucified. It is marked by the afternoon closing of certain businesses and offices. The next day, people around Hamburg build large bonfires to usher in the coming of spring. In the Black Forest and Westphalia, they set wheels afire and roll them down hills. Ancient beliefs say that if the wheels stay lighted to the bottom of the hill, there will be a good harvest. During the night, the *Osterhase* hops into town, hiding chocolate and nests of eggs for the children to discover on Easter morning. Egg hunting is followed by church services and feasting. Easter Monday is observed by the closing of businesses and government offices in many parts of the country.

A glowing Tannenbaum *in front of the town hall in Bonn. The tradition of decorating Christmas trees, now practiced by Christians all over the world, began in Germany.*

In the Rhineland and Bavaria, November 11 is St. Martin's Day, honoring the fourth-century patron saint of France. Known as a miracle worker in his lifetime, St. Martin is said to have torn his coat in two one day to give half to a beggar. The day is marked by processions of children carrying handmade paper lanterns led by a man on a white horse representing St. Martin. Following the parade, the children go door to door singing for treats.

Another centuries-old German tradition is the performance of the Oberammergau Passion Play. In the tiny town of Oberammergau, a performance has been staged every decade since 1680. Like all Europeans, the people of Oberammergau lived in grave fear of the Black Death that ravaged the continent for three centuries beginning in 1348. As the plague moved closer to Oberammergau in 1633, the people prayed fervently to God to spare them. God did. In grateful

A scene from the Passion Play, a religious theatrical performance that the tiny Bavarian town of Oberammergau has put on every decade for more than five hundred years.

thanks they composed a sixteen-act, five-and-a-half-hour play depicting the suffering and last days of Jesus Christ. It is staged outdoors in this Bavarian town at the start of each decade. More than a half million visitors come from around the world to watch the performance that involves fifteen hundred local people.

FOLK FESTIVALS

Germany's polycentrist growth is clearly reflected in the thousands of folk festivals celebrating everything from dragons to good harvests. *Drachenstich*, Bavaria's oldest folk festival, takes place each August in the little village of Fürth im Wald. *Drachenstich* dates back to the fifteenth century, when myth dictates that gallant knights slew dragons. The main event is a parade featuring a smoke- and fire-belching dragon being dragged through the streets to the accompaniment of brass bands and dancers.

The most elaborate harvest festivals are in the wine-producing regions of the Rhineland-Palatinate. During the first week in October, the *Weinlesefest* is held in Neustadt an der Weinstrasse. It is highlighted by a parade and the crowning of a wine queen. In late August and early September, the city of Mainz hosts the *Mainzer Weinmarkt*, a wine festival in the Volkspark, or "people's park."

In the same season, Worms on the Rhine celebrates *Backfischfest*, featuring baked fish accompanied by a good supply of wine. One of the highlights of the festival is *Fischerstechen*, a water contest in which competitors use long poles to knock each other off unstable flat-bottomed boats. The victor becomes "King of the River"; losers end up in the water.

The Rhine, Germany's river of fate that has seen and shaped so much of the country's history, is itself the subject of celebration in August and September. During *Rhein in Flammen*, the river lights up in a gorgeous fireworks festival. Riverside cities and towns stage spectacular fireworks displays that light up not only the water but the beautiful old castles tucked in the hillsides and the vineyards that line the terraced slopes along the river.

While the focal point of the Rhine festivals is wine, in Bavaria it is beer. In 1810, when Princess Therese von Sachsen-Hildburghausen became engaged to Bavarian prince Ludwig I, the entire population of Munich turned out to celebrate. Not surprisingly, in a region known for beer production, much of it was consumed at this event. So much did the people enjoy the party that it became a Munich tradition.

Partygoers enjoy carnival rides during Munich's sixteen-day Oktoberfest, *a traditional celebration famous for its beer, food, and festivities.*

Oktoberfest, as it is now called, is celebrated annually and attended by more than 6 million people from around the world. During the sixteen-day event, beginning in late September, they drink 1.3 million gallons (5 million liters) of beer, eat 750,000 chickens, and consume more than 500,000 German sausages.

Springtime is another season of festivals rooted in German history. May 1 is the day of Walpurga, the eighth-century saint believed to be a protector against magic. Legend says that on *Walpurgisnacht*, the evening of April 30, the devil held a feast for all his witches on the peak of the Brocken, the highest mountain in northern Germany. The modern-day Walpurgis Society, which started the festival, re-creates Walpurga's feast night with dancing and fireworks. When Germany was divided, the peak of the Brocken lay in communist

East Germany, forcing West Germans to hold their celebration on the western side of the mountain.

HONORING WRITERS AND MUSICIANS

Germany's many great musicians are memorialized in festivals throughout the country. One of the largest is the Wagner festival, honoring opera composer Richard Wagner. It is held in the Bavarian town of Bayreuth (BY-roit), where he lived, performed, and is buried. Each July since 1876, Wagner fans

THE LUDWIG-WAGNER-HITLER CONNECTION

Bavarian king Ludwig II was a great admirer of opera composer Richard Wagner and designed many of his castles around Wagnerian themes. He particularly loved *Lohengrin*, the tale of a mythical knight who descended to earth in a boat pulled by a magical swan. Near his castle Linderhof, Ludwig built a huge cave, the Blue Grotto. Envisioning himself as Lohengrin, he rode around the grotto's pond in a swan boat, carrying a sword at his side. Wagner's greatest masterpiece was *Der Ring des Nibelungen*, a series of four operas based on a thirteenth-century story poem called the *Nibelungenlied*. In it, the hero, Siegfried, is killed by those who fear his impending power. Wagner dedicated *Der Ring* to Ludwig, in gratitude for the king's financial help when he was struggling.

Adolf Hitler, born six years after Wagner died, admired the composer whose works he felt exalted the German spirit. Like Hitler, Wagner believed that Germans were destined to rule the world. Also like Hitler, Wagner hated Jews. He feared that their cleverness with money would lead to their worldwide control. In his opera *Rienzi*, a common citizen leads his people from the tyranny of wealthy lords and is later hailed as a king—a

hero Hitler unquestionably envisioned as himself. Wagnerian themes haunted Hitler in the final weeks of his rule. "*Die Götterdämmerung*," fourth opera in *Ring of the Nibelung*, means "Twilight of the Gods." Reporters and historians used the phrase to describe the last months of Hitler's reich as it neared collapse late in 1944 and early 1945.

German composer Richard Wagner

have trooped to Bayreuth for the festival. Three times daily, excerpts from his operas are played in the living room of his home, Wahrfried, which is now a museum. The focal point of the festival is the *Festspielhaus*, the plain but acoustically elegant building Wagner constructed for the performance of his grandiose operas.

German classical composer Ludwig von Beethoven is honored with a festival held every third year in September. The setting is his birthplace of Bonn, the capital of former West Germany. The festival is held in Beethoven's home, now a museum housing his last grand piano as well as some of the ear trumpets that aided him in his deafness.

Berlin is the scene of the Bach Festival in July, memorializing this family of fine musicians who brought honor to Germany in the seventeenth and eighteenth centuries. The father, Johann Sebastian, is best known for his religious music played on huge cathedral organs, but he also composed oratorios, preludes, cantatas, and fugues. Among his famous children, who were also accomplished musicians and composers, were Wilhelm Friedmann, Carl Philipp Emanuel, and Johann Christian Bach.

Austrian composer Mozart lived briefly in Germany, and his music is still celebrated with festivals in Dresden and Würzburg.

Although Wolfgang Amadeus Mozart was an Austrian composer, his life in Dresden, Germany, is celebrated there each May. The "Mozart's Heritage in Dresden Festival" features symphony and chamber music concerts as well as operatic performances. He is also remembered in a June festival in Würzburg, a Bavarian town that was nearly destroyed by bombing raids during World War II. Bavaria is also the venue for the Munich Opera Festival, whose National Theater is one of the most beautiful opera houses in the world. Hundreds of other festivals honoring more modern composers take place at locations around the country.

Weimar, birthplace of the ill-fated Weimar Republic, was home to two of Germany's finest writers. Johann Wolfgang von Goethe, the greatest of German poets, lived here in the late eighteenth and early nineteenth centuries. It was in Weimar, a town he turned into a major cultural center, that he wrote his masterpiece *Faust*. This poetic drama concerns a man who made a pact with the devil, Mephistopheles, in exchange for knowledge and favors.

Around the corner from Goethe lived his longtime friend Johann Friedrich von Schiller, known as Germany's greatest dramatist. Like Goethe, Schiller was multitalented and achieved great success as a poet, philosopher, and historian. Millions of visitors from around the world travel to Weimar to see the homes of these great German writers and to attend festivals honoring their works. The two are buried side by side in Weimar's Historischer Friedhof (Historic Cemetery).

HISTORY COMES ALIVE IN GERMAN MUSEUMS

The Goethehaus and museum, the Schillerhaus, the Beethovenhaus, the Festpielhaus are but a few of the thousands of interesting museums where German history comes to life. The Deutsches Museum in Munich chronicles the country's contributions to science and industry. Founded in 1903, it is located in a spectacular 1920s building that contains twelve miles of hallways. Its thousands of exhibits are organized into thirty departments representing different areas of science and industry.

The history of printing is explored in detail at the popular Gutenberg Museum in Mainz, the city where Johannes Gutenberg built the first press and invented movable type. Here, visitors can see a superb replica of the original printing press and an original of the Gutenberg Bible, one of only forty-seven remaining in the world.

Germany's artistic heritage is displayed in its many fine art museums and galleries. Hamburg's Kunsthalle houses one of the most impressive collections. Its three thousand paintings and four hundred sculptures include some of the finest works of European artists, from the fourteenth century to the present. Among the focal points of art in Berlin is the Gemäldegalerie, housing paintings of native artists such as Dürer and other world masters.

Graphic artist, draftsman, and sixteenth-century illustrator Lucas Cranach the Elder was famous not only for the quality but the speed of his work. More than four hundred of his paintings are known to exist, a few of them displayed in the Gemäldegalerie, but that is only a fraction of what he produced. Lucas's son, the Younger, was also a famous painter. The works of another of the sixteenth-century greats,

STURM UND DRANG

Master writers Johann Friedrich von Schiller and Johann Wolfgang von Goethe became famous during the German literary revolution known as *Sturm und Drang*. "Storm and Stress," which reached its height during the 1770s, was a time for glorifying nature and writing of the individualism of the human spirit. The heroes were uncommon people with strong personalities who used their strengths to defy the traditional world. Heroes were sometimes good, sometimes bad, but they were always in conflict with society. Many of Schiller's heroes were historic figures of the past, like legendary marksman William Tell and Mary Queen of Scots. These characters were caught in a moral tug of war between duty and desire. They rejected traditional authority and triumphed because of their special strengths and tenacious spirits.

Goethe's first novel, *The Sorrows of Young Werther*, which involves his own sorrowful love affair, became a hallmark of *Sturm und Drang*. Like many other writers of this movement, Goethe relied on German characters and topics for his stories, rather than on foreign subjects. In his most famous work, the hero Faust is an intellectual torn between idealism and materialism.

Master composer Ludwig von Beethoven was also creating during *Sturm und Drang*. Believing strongly in a person's God-given right to freedom, Beethoven chose Schiller's poem "Ode to Joy" as the finale for his *Ninth Symphony*. In it the singers proclaim, "All mankind are brothers."

Hans Holbein the Younger, are also on display at the Gemälde-galerie. One of the greatest portrait artists of all time, Holbein became famous painting court scenes for King Henry VIII of England.

A darker side of German history is recalled in two restored concentration camps from the Hitler era. Dachau, first of the Nazi camps, is located twenty minutes from Munich. The public may tour the grounds where the barracks were located and visit a museum recording the horror of the concentration camp system. Just outside Weimar is Buchenwald, another restored camp. The thirty-five-thousand-plus people who were killed there are remembered by thirty-five thousand small stones, placed where the long rows of barracks used to be. On the highest point of ground within the camp, a long wide set of stairs leads to a tower, erected in condemnation of the unspeakable horror that occurred here and in other camps around the reich.

The days of Germany's division during the cold war are chronicled at Berlin's Haus am Checkpoint Charlie (the Wall Museum), where the Berlin Wall stood for four decades, dividing the city, the country, and the world. Visitors can learn the history of the Berlin Wall's construction and demise, and view some of the tools and methods that East Germans used to escape to the west—among them a miniature submarine.

PALACES AND CASTLES

Castles reminiscent of kings, queens, and fairy tales dot the German countryside, taking visitors back to medieval and imperial times. The gem of Berlin is Schloss Charlottenburg, which has been compared to French king Louis XIV's palace at Versailles. This exquisite abode served as the living quarters of various Prussian kings. Begun in 1695 by Frederick I, it was improved and expanded by subsequent rulers including Frederick the Great. A Baroque-style statue of Frederick William, the Great Elector, peers down from the elaborate courtyard. Several museums within the palace feature artifacts from the time periods of its inhabitants. Among them is the barren crown of Frederick (II) the Great, who took from it all the valuable jewels to give to his wife.

Frederick II also kept an elegant summer home, Schloss Sanssouci, in the Berlin suburb of Potsdam. Although much of the palace was destroyed in bombing raids during World War II, it has since been restored. Construction of Sanssouci, meaning "without a care," was begun by Frederick's father, Friedrich Wilhelm I. Later it was expanded in the Rococo style of lavish ornamentation—at great expense to the king and his subjects. Today Sanssouci's 5 million annual visitors stroll the gardens and visit the five rooms where Frederick the Great stayed while he was in residence. Also open for view are the rooms he kept for guests such as Johann Sebastian Bach and the French philosopher Voltaire. Both Frederick II and his father are buried on the grounds.

Much older than the *Schlösser* of the Prussian kings were the castles owned by the great land barons of the Middle Ages. One of those is Wartburg Castle in Eisenach, begun in 1067. In its halls performed the great minstrels of the Middle Ages.

The grandest of its performance areas, the ornate thirteenth-century Great Hall, is open to the public. Over the centuries, many historic figures spent time at Wartburg, among them Goethe, Martin Luther, and Johann Sebastian Bach.

In contrast to the castles of great leaders are the fairy tale castles of central Germany and Bavaria. Germany has an "official" 350-kilometer fairy tale road that stretches from Bremerhaven to Hanau, near Frankfurt. Hanau was the home of the brothers Jacob and Wilhelm Grimm, creators of literary witches, castles, and fairy tales. The road offers a breathtaking view of towering cathedrals, turreted castles, and walled towns.

In the mountains of Bavaria are the castles of King Ludwig II, called "Mad" Ludwig because his subjects considered him crazy. Ludwig devoted a great deal of time and his subjects' money to building elaborate fairy tale castles. Linderhof, the only one completed during his lifetime, has rooms like jewels, decorated with gargantuan amounts of gold, marble, and crystal chandeliers. For ease in serving large

An aerial photo of the stately Schloss Charlottenburg, built from 1695 to 1699 in Berlin, reveals the elegant garden designs behind the palace and a statue of Frederick William in the front courtyard.

banquets, the massive dining room table could be lowered into the kitchens on the sublevel, set with food, and raised ready for feasting.

Ludwig spent much of his boyhood at Schwangau, meaning "swan region," in southwestern Bavaria. Directly across the valley from Hohenschwangau, the royal castle that was his home, Ludwig chose the spot for his dream castle, Neuschwanstein. Seventeen years in the making, Neuschwanstein became the inspiration for the castle at Walt Disney's Magic Kingdom and for Sleeping Beauty's castle in the Disney movie. A masterpiece of design and construction, Neuschwanstein's focal point is a two-story throne room. It features a sky-blue ceiling glittering with stars, gold walls, and a mosaic tile floor designed with plants and animals. On the wall, an elaborate painting shows Christ floating amid kings and disciples. But alas, the spectacular throne room

HISTORIC GATES AND WALLED CITIES

Since its founding in 1040, Nuremberg has played a major role in German history. Its ancient architecture, much of it devastated in bombing raids during World War II, has been reconstructed and stands today as a reminder of its historic past. Enclosing the old city, or Altstadt, are ancient walls completed in 1452 containing huge gates, watchtowers, and moats. Along the cobblestone streets, craftsmen dressed in Middle Ages garb create and sell crafts of that era, such as puppets, pewter mugs, and plates.

The city is alive with Gothic architecture and spectacular cathedrals. In the marketplace stands the Schöner Brunnen (Beautiful Fountain), a sixty-foot Gothic sculpture carved about 1400. In the tower of the 1350s Frauenkirche (Church of Our Holy Lady), a clock strikes every day at noon. It ushers out figures representing the electors of the empire who bow to Emperor Charles IV, then retreat into the clockworks until noon the next day.

Perhaps the most spectacular architecture in the city is the Kaiserburg, or Imperial Castle. This complex of buildings was the home of the Holy Roman emperors beginning in 1050. It is filled with ornate and craggy structures such as the Renaissance era Doppelkappelle (Double Chapel).

Crowned by the Goddess of Peace driving a chariot pulled by four horses, Brandenburg Gate in Berlin was built as an arch of triumph for Frederick Wilhelm II and became a symbol for German unity in 1990.

has no throne, for Ludwig was declared insane and died— apparently a murder or suicide—before the throne could be completed.

But of all the great architecture that reflects the soul and character of Germany, none is more meaningful to its history than Brandenburger Tor in Berlin. Built between 1788 and 1791 as an arch of triumph for King Frederick Wilhelm II and victorious armies, Brandenburg is the only one of fourteen original arches still standing. On its top is a chariot with four horses, driven by the Goddess of Peace. In 1945, Brandenburg Gate became a symbol of shame when victorious Soviet troops marched through it to conquer Berlin. For the next four decades it stood as a symbol of Germany's defeat and division. Its purpose as an arch of triumph was at last recognized again in 1990 when the Berlin Wall was torn down and Germany was reunited. Today Brandenburger Tor stands as a symbol of German unity.

GERMAN CONTRIBUTIONS TO THE WORLD

The clarinet, the pocket watch, gun castings, geographic globes—these and other commonplace items in our culture were all invented in one German city, Nuremberg. During the Middle Ages, this city was the traffic hub of Europe. After World War II it became the world center for the toy industry. Nuremberg's achievements are only a small part of the contributions that Germans and Germany have made to the world in every field, from rocket science to classical music.

INDUSTRIAL AND SCIENTIFIC CONTRIBUTIONS

The most famous physicist of all time, Albert Einstein, was born in Ulm, Germany, in 1879. His genius developed the famous theory of relativity and its formula, $E=mc^2$. This discovery made it possible for scientists to build the atomic bomb. But Einstein was a German Jew whose genius could not save him from Adolf Hitler's rampant anti-Semitism. Nazi Germany's loss was America's gain when, in 1940, Einstein became a U.S. citizen. Fellow twentieth-century scientist Wernher von Braun developed a rocket-propelled bomb used successfully by the Germans during World War II. Von Braun immigrated to the United States after the war and developed the first U.S. satellite, *Explorer 1*, which was launched in 1958.

Another German-born physicist whose name became a household word was Daniel Gabriel Fahrenheit. This eighteenth-century scientist was the first to use mercury thermometers as precise measures of temperature. One of the worldwide temperature scales was named for him. World-renowned German mathematician and astronomer Johannes Kepler (1571–1630) discovered the basic rules of gravity. His findings showed how planets revolve in orbit around the sun. Another German scientist, Paul Ehrlich (1854–1915), studied disease-causing bacteria. Ehrlich led the way to finding cures for communicable diseases such as diphtheria. He was also the first to develop and use chemotherapy in treating cancer.

One of the major industrial innovations to sweep the world was the German *Volkswagen,* or "people's car." Developed in 1934, the VW "bug" was promoted by Adolf Hitler as an affordable car for all Germans. People could purchase inexpensive government savings stamps each week and at the end of four years would have enough to buy one of the little black cars. Unfortunately war got in the way of the purchase plan, but Volkswagens became a lasting addition to the automotive world. Anticipating increased traffic on German highways as more families owned cars, Hitler introduced the autobahn (literally "auto path"). This was a system of four-lane high-speed roads that stretched across the country. The autobahn became the model for cross-country highway systems in many nations.

SOCIAL AND CULTURAL CONTRIBUTIONS

Germany can thank writers like Schiller and Goethe and composers like Beethoven and Bach for its sobriquet "nation of poets and thinkers." With other talented Germans, they left their marks not only upon their country, but upon the world. One such composer was Georg Friedrich Handel, born the same year as Johann Sebastian Bach, in 1685. Handel composed the world's best-known musical oratorio, *Messiah.* Performed today in thousands of churches worldwide, it is easily recognized by its famous "Hallelujah Chorus."

Nineteenth-century German composers Felix Mendelssohn and Robert Schumann made great contributions to the early Romantic period of music. Mendelssohn's best-known work is the concert overture to *A Midsummer Night's Dream.* Schumann is remembered for his fresh, youthful contributions to the *Lieder,* among the greatest of German art songs. Also a music critic, he was among the first to hear and promote composer Johannes Brahms, famous for his lullabies and for *Hungarian Dances.*

The land of thinkers was fortunate to claim eighteenth-century philosopher Immanuel Kant. Before Kant, philosophers held that all knowledge

German scientist Wernher von Braun immigrated to the United States after World War II.

was merely experience, that the human mind was nothing but a clean slate on which to record one's experiences. Kant rejected that idea. He claimed that the human mind is the source of knowledge and that it organizes experiences into further knowledge. His beliefs are contained in his *Critique of Pure Reason*, which has become a classic.

A political movement that would eventually consume large parts of Asia and eastern Europe began in Germany in the mid–nineteenth century. German socialists Karl Marx and Friedrich Engels were known as the fathers of modern communism. Their *Communist Manifesto* showed how common people could attain power by participating in revolutions against the government. Marx also became famous for his book *Das Kapital*, which discusses the conflict between the wealthy and the poor working class.

Composer Georg Friedrich Handel's most famous work, the oratorio Messiah, *was first performed in 1742.*

One of Germany's most important social contributions to the world was kindergarten. Not only is *Kindergarten* a German word ("children's garden"), the entire educational concept is German. This system for educating four- to six-year-olds was developed in Blankenburg, Germany, in 1837 by teacher Friedrich Froebel. His goal was to teach young children through play. He chose the word *garten* for he believed that in this environment, children would grow like flowers in a garden.

THE GREAT GERMAN LITERARY HERITAGE

Thomas Mann, born in 1875, is considered one of the greatest writers of the twentieth century. One of Mann's common themes was the problems artists encounter in dealing with the business world. He is best known for *The Magic Mountain*, which explores the spiritual development of a tuberculosis patient. The young man forms his view of the world by listening to other patients in the sanitorium discuss ideas and problems of the day. Outspoken against the Nazis, Mann immigrated to the United States and became a citizen in 1944.

Immanuel Kant (1724–1804), German philosopher and author of Critique of Pure Reason.

Mann's contemporary Hermann Hesse was, like Mann, a Nobel Prize winner. His novels explore man's escape from conventional lifestyles to find one's true spirit. A romantic and lover of nature, Hesse became a follower of Eastern mysticism, which led to his masterwork *Siddharta*, based on the life of Buddha. He also gained fame through his novels *Demian* and *Der Steppenwolf.*

Two German writers whose lives and works were deeply affected by war both served as soldiers in World War I. So devastated was Bertolt Brecht by his wartime experiences that he became a pacifist. This poet, dramatist, and theatrical producer later rejected all conventional themes in his writing. His major theatrical success, written with the German composer Kurt Weill, was *The Threepenny Opera*, which explores the social conditions that force people into a life of crime. Novelist Erich Maria Remarque made war the theme of his famous classic work *All Quiet on the Western Front.* The book is considered one of the finest personal accounts of war ever written.

Germany's history of producing exceptional literature continued into the twentieth century with great writers such as Thomas Mann (pictured), Hermann Hesse, Erich Maria Remarque, and Heinrich Böll.

After the fall of the Nazi regime, few German writers, artists, or common citizens were anxious to speak out on the subject. The horrors of Hitler's Third Reich were too painful or too humiliating to write about in the immediate postwar years. A notable exception was novelist Heinrich Böll, who served in the German army throughout the war and later wrote intimately of life in Hitler's Germany. A Nobel Prize winner, Böll's best-known stories of war are *Wo warst du Adam?* and *The Train Was on Time.* Another postwar author, Günter Grass, became the spokesman for an entire generation of disillusioned young Germans. His greatest novel, *The Tin Drum,* shows how Nazi influence crept into the average family. Grass also paints a detailed picture of the devastating toll taken by the war in Germany and the economic miracle that occurred after the country's defeat.

A LEGACY OF SHAME, A FUTURE OF HOPE

Despite its millennium of rich cultural and political history, the definitive events in the shaping of modern Germany took place in the twentieth century. Without doubt, the blackest years of German history were those of the Third Reich, when unspeakable atrocities were committed by a government that had the support of the German people. Regardless of their involvement, postwar Germans have had to bear a measure of pain and guilt. Says former Hitler Youth leader Alfons Heck, in his book *The Burden of Hitler's Legacy:*

> The Hitler era with its roughly 50 million casualties was much more than a Jewish tragedy. It is an indictment of all humanity, which has left me with a lasting skepticism about the innate goodness of man.

Yet in the last half of the twentieth century, Germany has rebounded from the devastation of war and the amputation of its five eastern states by a communist regime to become one of the strongest members of the European community. Horror and shame have been replaced by success and optimism. Prior to unification, many people feared that a united Germany might become a militaristic Germany. Those fears have thus far proved baseless. Says Eric Solsten in his book *Germany: A Country Study*, "In the postwar era Germany has steadfastly worked [toward] Thomas Mann's ideal of a Europeanized Germany and rejected his nightmare of a Germanized Europe." On its present course, Germany promises to uphold Mann's ideal into the twenty-first century.

FACTS ABOUT GERMANY

GOVERNMENT

Form of government: Federal Republic, made up of sixteen states and headed by a president. Bicameral parliament (no official name) consists of an upper house, the Federal Council, or *Bundesrat*, in which the states are represented; lower house is the Federal Diet, or *Bundestag*. Constitution is the Basic Law, adopted May 23, 1949.

Date of independence: First unification of the German Empire: January 18, 1871. Following World War II, Germany was divided for nearly forty-five years into two countries, East and West Germany. On October 3, 1990, the two were again united.

National anthem: Third stanza of *Lied der Deutschen*, "Song of Germany," with text by August Heinrich Hoffmann von Fallersleben (1789–1874) and music by Joseph Hayden (1732–1809).

National flag: One each of black, red, and gold bars stacked horizontally top to bottom; the colors are said to represent the German qualities of freedom and liberalism. These colors were first used as a national symbol after 1918, with the birth of the Weimar Republic.

Major political parties:
Christian Democratic Union (CDU)/Christian Social Union
    (Chancellor Helmut Kohl's party)
Social Democratic Party
Free Democratic Party (a coalition with Kohl's CDU party)
Alliance '90/Greens
Party of Democratic Socialism

NATIONAL HOLIDAYS

January 1	New Year's
January 6	Epiphany
variable	Good Friday, Easter Sunday and Monday
May 1	Labor Day
variable	Ascension Day, Whitsunday, and Pentecost Monday
variable	Corpus Christi (southern Germany only)
October 3	German Unity Day
November 1	All Saints' Day
variable	Day of Prayer and Repentance
December 24–26	Christmas

POPULATION

Comparative population (in millions)

1850 .... 35.3		1930 .... 65.1
1860 .... 37.6		1940 .... 69.9
1870 .... 40.8		1950 .... 68.4*
1880 .... 45.1		1960 .... 72.7
1890 .... 49.2		1970 .... 77.7
1900 .... 56.0		1980 .... 78.3
1910 .... 64.6		1990 .... 79.4
1920 .... 61.8*		

(*Declines due to World Wars I and II, respectively; post–World War II figures include both East and West Germany through the period of division)

Population of major cities:
Berlin: 3.47 million
Hamburg: 1.7 million
Munich: 1.25 million
Cologne: 964,000
Frankfurt am Main: 652,000
Essen: 617,000
Dortmund: 601,000
Stuttgart: 589,000
Düsseldorf: 573,000
Bremen: 549,000

PEOPLE

Total population: 81.8 million

Average annual growth rate: 2%

Birthrate: 9.46 per 1,000 (world average: 26 per 1,000)

Death rate: 11.2 per 1,000

Infant mortality rate: 5.9 per 1,000

Life expectancy: 73 years male; 79 years female

Marriage rate: 6.5 per 1,000

Female population: 42 million

Male population: 39.8 million

Percentage of population 14 yrs. and under: 16.8%

Percentage of population over age 65: 14.9%

Foreign workers: 7.2 million

Population density: 585 people per sq. mi. (229 people per sq. km.)

Ethnic breakdown: German, 95.1%; Turkish, 2.3%; Italian, 0.7%; Greek, 0.4%; Polish, 0.4%; Other, 1.1% (primarily refugees from former Yugoslavia)

Literacy rate: 98%

Religious affiliations: 55.2 million practicing Christians: 28.2 million Protestants; 27 million Roman Catholics. Remainder are unaffiliated or belong to small denominations. Percentages: 45% Protestant; 37% Roman Catholic; 18% unaffiliated or other

Major language: German

Educational levels attained: primary school, 100%; secondary school, 97%; postsecondary education, 32%

GEOGRAPHY

Land area: 137,826 sq. mi.(356,854 sq. km.)

Highest point: Zugspitze, 9,721 ft. (2,963 m.)

Lowest point: Riepsterhammerich, 6.5 ft. below sea level (2 m.)

Longest rivers (their distances within Germany):
Rhine: 537 mi. (865 km.)
Elbe: 435 mi. (700 km.)
Danube: 426 mi. (686 km.)

Largest lake: Constance (*Bodensee*), 118 sq. mi. (305 sq. km.)

Forested land: nearly ⅓ of the total area of the country, 10.4 million hectares

Coastline: 1,290 mi. (2,389 km.)

Land use: arable land, 34%; forest and woodland, 30%; meadow and pasture, 16%; other, 20%

Recycling practices: Germans recycle 47% of waste paper, 70% of used tires, 75% of glass, according to color

CLIMATE

Average annual temperature: 48° F (9° C)

Average January temperature: 22°– 30° F (-6°– -1° C)

Average July temperature: 63°– 68° F (17°– 20° C)

Average annual rainfall: about 20 inches per year

ECONOMY

Currency: deutsche mark; DM 1 = 100 Pfennigs; DM 1.76 = $1.00 U.S.

Economic system: social market economy

Major industries: automotive, mechanical engineering, electrical engineering, chemical and pharmaceutical, iron and steel

Foreign trade: approximate annual imports, DM 635 billion; exports DM 730 billion

Gross domestic product: $5,308.05 billion

Labor force: 34.5 million

Unemployment: West, 9%; East, 15.7%

CHRONOLOGY

1st Century
Teutonic tribes inhabit present-day western Germany;
Romans expand their empire north to the Danube River

38
City of Cologne (*Köln*) settled by the Romans

ca. 0–486
Various tribes inhabit central Europe, among them Franks,
Saxons, Swabians, and Bavarians; from outside the area
come the Visigoths, Vandals, and Huns, barbaric tribes who
stage repeated attacks

9
Arminius, prince of the Cherusci tribe, said to have de-
feated three legions of Roman soldiers in the Teutoburg
Forest of northwest Germany

433
Attila takes command of the Huns and overpowers other
tribes of central Europe

451
Near Orleans, Attila's army is defeated for the first and
only time

486
Clovis, leader of the Franks, defeats the last of the Roman
governors then ruling present-day Germany

500
By the start of the sixth century, the tribes roaming Germany have united into three main groups: Franks, Saxons,
and Alemanni

742
Charlemagne (Charles the Great), son of Pépin, believed to
have been born near present-day Aachen

751
Pépin the Short becomes king of the Franks

768
Pépin dies; Charlemagne becomes king of the northern Franks

800
Pope Leo III crowns Charlemagne "Emperor of the Romans," the first ruler of the future Holy Roman Empire

814
Charlemagne dies, and his empire begins to crumble

843
Treaty of Verdun is signed, dividing France and Germany into separate countries

911
The year many historians consider the official beginning of German history; Conrad I, duke of Franconia, is crowned first real German king

919
Conrad I dies; Henry I named successor

ca. 919–949
German society sheds its tribal division and becomes organized under feudalism

936
Henry I dies; his son, Otto I (Otto the Great), is elected king—Otto is first ruler to think of Germany as a nation, rather than a group of independent duchies

962
Otto the Great crowned emperor by the pope; First German Reich ("empire") begins

Early 1100s
Businessmen begin to organize into guilds

1138–1254
Hohenstaufen dynasty rules Germany, expanding its territory, developing domestic skills, and enhancing cultural life; Holy Roman Empire reaches its peak of power

1152
Frederick Barbarossa (Red Beard), considered the greatest of Hohenstaufen rulers, begins his reign as king of Germany

1155
Frederick I adds the word *holy* to Roman Empire

1190
Frederick I dies leading the Third Crusade to free Jerusalem

1215
Frederick I's grandson Frederick II, one of the greatest Hohenstaufen rulers and a patron of the arts and learning, becomes king of Germany

1223
Frederick II crowned Holy Roman emperor

1228
Frederick II undertakes Crusade that brings Holy Lands under his control and makes him king of Jerusalem

1239
After a stormy relationship, Frederick II splits with the pope and is excommunicated

1256–1273
The Great Interregnum, during which time Germany had no emperor nor any strong leaders in the states

1273
The Great Interregnum comes to an end with the crowning of Rudolf, first of the Habsburg emperors

ca. 1299
Formation of the Hanseatic League, an organization of cities whose goal is to protect traders and merchants from pirates and robbers as well as from unfair competition; continued until 1669

1300s
The Black Death, a disease brought by traders from China, claims the lives of 25 million Europeans

1411
The Hohenzollern dynasty, known for its loyalty to the Holy Roman emperors, begins to gain influence

1440
Frederick V, a Habsburg ruler, takes the throne of Germany, becoming the Holy Roman emperor Frederick III twelve years later

ca. 1440
Johannes Gutenberg develops movable type and the printing press, making possible the mechanical reproduction of books

1456
First mechanical reproduction of the Bible printed on Gutenberg presses

1468
Gutenberg, whose printing inventions revolutionized the world, dies broke and nearly blind

1517
Theology professor Martin Luther posts on the door of the Castle Church in Wittenberg his ninety-five theses concerning the sale of indulgences, which launches the Reformation, the sixteenth-century religious revolution resulting in the birth of Protestantism

1521
Emperor Charles V commands Luther to appear before the Diet of Worms to recant his statements concerning the church; Luther refuses

1530
Luther and his followers create the Augsburg Confession, a statement of twenty-one articles of the emerging Protestant faith, claiming that the Bible, not church authorities, is the final word on religious matters; their break from Catholicism would never be reversed

1547
Charles V goes to war against the Protestant princes, but finds the mission fruitless and turns over the reins of German government to his brother, Ferdinand

1555
Ferdinand declares the Peace of Augsburg, allowing the princes in the various German states to decide on the religion to be followed in their region; half of Germany becomes Protestant

1572
Martin Luther's campaign to remove Jews from Germany "for all time" is successful, and they are banned by the government from remaining in or returning to the country

1618
Holy Roman Emperor Ferdinand II of Austria declares war on Frederick, Protestant ruler of Bohemia, launching the Thirty Years' War, a largely religious and very bloody series

of encounters that takes the lives of a quarter to a third of the German people

1640
Frederick William (the Great Elector) becomes elector of Brandenburg, the area surrounding Berlin

1648
After a series of ineffective truces, the Peace of Westphalia is signed, ending the Thirty Years' War; Germany gains religious freedom and the already wounded Holy Roman Empire becomes even weaker

1660
Prussia breaks away from Poland, under Frederick's leadership and strengthened army

1701
Frederick I, son of the Great Elector and a prolific spender, becomes first king of Prussia

1740
Frederick II (Frederick the Great) becomes king of Prussia, and attacks Austria and Silesia to make Prussia a major world power

1772
With allies Russia and Austria, Frederick captures a third of Poland, the First Partition of that country

1786
Frederick the Great's reign ends

1795
Following two more partitions by Prussia and other European powers, Poland is wiped off maps of the world for the next 123 years

1806
The Prussian army is crushed by Napoleon Bonaparte at Jena (modern Thuringia), causing the new king, Frederick William III, to lose nearly half his kingdom, which marks the end of the First German Reich and the Holy Roman Empire

1813
With Austria and Russia, Prussia defeats Napoleon at the Battle of Leipzig; two years later the great French general meets his final downfall at Waterloo in Belgium

1814–1815
The Congress of Vienna meets to restore order to chaotic
Europe and establishes the German Confederation, made
up of thirty-eight states and four independent cities

1862
Otto von Bismarck is made chancellor of Prussia and
promises to unite the German nation by force

1870
Bismarck provokes the Franco-Prussian War with France,
a move intended to bind southern Germany with Prussia
against a common enemy

1871
All German states except Austria are united as the "German
Empire," beginning the Second Reich, ruled technically
by Kaiser (Emperor) Wilhelm I, but with Bismarck as
its true leader

1888
William II becomes emperor of Prussia and Bismarck's
power wanes

1898
Otto von Bismarck, the Iron Chancellor, dies

1914
On August 1, following the June 28 assassination of Arch-
duke Francis Ferdinand, heir to the throne of Austria-
Hungary, World War I begins; historians blame Kaiser
Wilhelm II as the primary perpetrator, citing his pursuit
of the image of the ironclad Prussian leader

1918
On November 11, the armistice ending World War I is
signed; Germany is defeated and Kaiser Wilhelm flees the
country; worldwide, 8.5 million people are dead and 21
million wounded as a result of the war

1919
An assembly of elected representatives meets in February
in the city of Weimar to draw up a new government, the
Weimar Republic, which proves to be weak and ineffective;
on June 28, the Treaty of Versailles is signed in France, out-
lining the terms by which Germany and the other nations
defeated in World War I must abide; the terms for Germany
are exceedingly harsh

1920
On February 24, more than two thousand disaffected German citizens meet at the *Hofbräuhaus* in Munich to listen to Adolf Hitler, representative of a new political party, refute the hated Treaty of Versailles

1932
Elections show that 14 million Germans now support Adolf Hitler and the Nazi Party

1933
On January 30, German president Paul von Hindenburg unwillingly accedes to Hitler's demands to make him chancellor, marking the beginning of the Third Reich; though Hitler predicted it would last one thousand years, it lasted only twelve, and brought unending shame upon the German nation

1934
Hitler orders the killing of his enemies in the Nazi Party in a series of bloody events in late June known variously as the Blood Purge, Night of the Long Knives, or Röhm Purge, named after Ernst Röhm, leader of the storm troopers, known as the *Sturm Abteilung* (SA) or Brownshirts, who is among the victims

1935
Passage of the Nuremberg Laws in September severely restricts the rights of German Jews

1936
On March 7, Hitler's troops take back the Rhineland from France in a bloodless conquest

1938
On March 12, German troops invade Austria, accomplishing the *Anschluss*—the reunification of the Germanic peoples; on October 1, German troops invade the Sudetenland in Czechoslovakia; on November 9–10 is *Kristallnacht*, "Night of Broken Glass," an onslaught of violence directed at the German Jews by the Nazis—Jewish businesses and synagogues are destroyed and Jews shipped to concentration camps

1939
At 5:45 A.M. on September 1, German troops attack Poland, igniting World War II

1940
On June 14, France falls to the Germans; from July to September, the Battle of Britain rages between the air forces of

England and Germany, but the Germans eventually return home without a victory; on September 27, Italy and Japan enter into a ten-year military and economic agreement, forging the Axis alliance

1941
Operation Barbarossa, the German invasion of the Soviet Union, begins on June 22

1942
The Wannsee Conference to draw up plans for the Final Solution, the Nazis' plan to exterminate the Jews of Europe, takes place in the Berlin suburb of Wannsee on January 20

1943
German troops surrender at Stalingrad in February, defeated in Operation Barbarossa

1944
The D Day invasion of Europe by Allied troops begins on June 6; the attempted assassination of Adolf Hitler by his own generals takes place on July 20; the Battle of the Bulge, Germany's last major attack of the war, occurs on December 16

1945
Hitler marries his longtime mistress, Eva Braun, on April 29; the next day they commit suicide in his underground bunker in Berlin; Germany surrenders to Allied forces on May 7, ending World War II in Europe; July 17– August 2, Allied leaders meet near Berlin for the Potsdam Conference to divide Germany into four zones of occupation

1946–1947
Relations between the democratic government of West Germany and the communist government of East Germany begin to deteriorate, paving the way for the cold war

1948
In response to the Russians' cutting off all access into the city of Berlin, Allied pilots begin an air drop of food, fuel, and supplies on June 26

1949
Popular leader Konrad Adenauer becomes the first chancellor of West Germany; Walter Ulbricht becomes deputy prime minister of East Germany, bringing to it a harsh form of socialism and banning any political parties that

do not agree with him; on May 4 the Soviets at last lift
the blockade of Berlin, but the cold war has become much
colder

1950s
More East Germans try to escape their repressive communist government by fleeing to West Germany

1961
With the number of East German escapees at 3.5 million,
on August 13 the communists begin building the Berlin
Wall, a twenty-eight-mile concrete and barbed wire barrier
dividing East and West Berlin, symbolically dividing the
communist world from the free world

1971
Repressive communist leader Erich Honecker becomes
general secretary of East Germany's Socialist Unity Party
and rules the country with an iron hand

1972
Diplomatic relations established between East and West
Germany—leaders of the two countries are at last speaking
to each other

1972–1989
The cold war begins to thaw, aided by Soviet leader
Mikhail Gorbachev's advancement of *perestroika* and
glasnost

1982
Helmut Kohl, the man who will lead Germany toward unification, becomes chancellor

1989
On October 7, during celebrations marking the fortieth anniversary of the East German government, demonstrations
against Honecker result in his removal from office; on November 9, the communist government at last reopens the
Berlin Wall after twenty-eight years of repression

1990
After forty-one years of being divided, Germany again becomes one country during unification on October 3

1992
The Treaty on the European Union is signed February 7;
Germany is one of its major members

Suggestions for Further Reading

Eleanor H. Ayer, *Exploring Cultures of the World: Germany, in the Heartland of Europe.* Tarrytown, NY: Marshall Cavendish, 1996. Colorfully illustrated introduction to the geography, history, people, festivals, food, school, and culture of Germany.

———, *The Holocaust Library: The Survivors.* San Diego, CA: Lucent Books, 1997. Follows Holocaust survivors from their liberation in the concentration and death camps through emigration, rebirth, renewal, and the founding of Israel.

———, *The Importance of Adolf Hitler.* San Diego, CA: Lucent Books, 1996. In-depth look at the megalomaniacal leader who led the German nation into World War II and the Holocaust.

David Flint, *On the Map: Germany.* Austin, TX: Raintree-Steck Vaughn, 1994. A thirty-four-page overview of German geography, history, and culture.

Barbara Fuller, *Cultures of the World: Germany.* Tarrytown, NY: Marshall Cavendish, 1995. Includes statistics, geography, and information on social issues, government, economy, history, arts, customs, education, food, and sports. 128 pages, illustrated in full color.

Anita Ganeri, *Focus on Germany and the Germans.* New York: Gloucester Press, 1993. A thirty-four-page look at the country and the German people.

Diane Yancey, *The Reunification of Germany.* San Diego, CA: Lucent Books, 1994. A look at the events leading up to unification, the methods and means used for uniting the two countries, and prospects for the future.

WORKS CONSULTED

Timothy Garton Ash, *In Europe's Name: Germany and the Divided Continent*. New York: Random House, 1993. Describes in detail the effort, money, and diplomacy that went into the unification process as well as the struggles encountered before it finally succeeded.

Eleanor H. Ayer, *Cities at War: Berlin*. New York: Maxwell Macmillan, 1992. Life in Germany's capital city during World War II, as experienced by the teenagers who were living there, in hiding there, or serving in the armed forces. Includes postwar events through unification.

————, *World Partners: Germany*. Vero Beach, FL: Rourke Corporation, 1990. Explores postwar Germany, the cold war, the European community, unification, and the future of Germany.

Berlin in Brief. Berlin: Presse-und Informationsamt of the Federal State of Berlin, 1995. A sixty-four-page book covering the history and geography of the city/state, as well as current topics in education, finance, regional planning, housing, science, culture, and politics. Profusely illustrated with photos, graphs, and charts.

Borgna Brunner, ed., *1998 Information Please Almanac*. Boston: Information Please LLC, 1997. "Countries of the World" section contains information on German history, geography, government, economics, population, and ethnicity.

George Constable, ed., *Library of Nations: Germany*. N.p.: Time-Life Books, 1984. A 160-page book of picture essays and text describing the history, geography, economy, and culture of the German nation.

Gordon A. Craig, *The Germans*. New York: G. P. Putnam's Sons, 1982. A professor of German history assesses the topics of

Germans and Jews, money, religion, women, soldiers, politics, and historical perspectives.

Eugene Davidson, *The Making of Adolf Hitler*. New York: Macmillan, 1977. Hitler's early life and rise to power from 1889 to 1933.

Daniel Goldhagen, *Hitler's Willing Executioners*. New York: Alfred Knopf, 1996. Places the blame for complicity in the Holocaust on the entire German nation, not merely on its Nazi leaders.

Robert Goralski, *World War II Almanac 1931–1945*. New York: Bonanza Books, 1981. A complete chronology of the war with photographs, maps, graphs, and tables.

Alfons Heck, *The Burden of Hitler's Legacy*. Frederick, CO: Renaissance House, 1988. Autobiography of a former Hitler Youth leader, telling of his service in the Third Reich and the subsequent soul-searching he has done regarding Germany's role in World War II and the Holocaust.

Paul Johnson, *A History of the Jews*. New York: Harper & Row, 1987. A complete history of the Jewish people, from the time of the ancient Israelites to the present.

Arno Kappler, ed., *Facts About Germany*. Frankfurt am Main: Societäts-Verlag, 1996. A 550-page book containing up-to-date information on German economic, political, and cultural life as well as history and geography, endorsed by the German government and distributed by the German Information Agency.

H. W. Koch, *A History of Prussia*. New York: Dorset Press, 1978. A 326-page account of the geography, politics, leadership, and culture of Prussia.

David Low, ed., *Affordable Germany*. New York: Fodor's Travel Publications, 1993. A guidebook to contemporary and historical sites and museums in Germany.

David Marsh, *The Germans: A People at the Crossroads*. New York: St. Martin's Press, 1989. An in-depth look at the German people on the eve of unification and an assessment of the future of a united Germany.

Earle Rice Jr., *The Holocaust Library: The Final Solution.* San Diego, CA: Lucent Books, 1997. Explores the roots of genocide, Jewish life in Nazi Germany, the Special Killing Forces, and the implementation of the Final Solution, the extermination of European Jewry.

William L. Shirer, *The Rise and Fall of the Third Reich.* New York: Simon & Schuster, 1960. A 1,250-page study of Nazi Germany by its premier historian.

Eric Solsten, *Germany: A Country Study.* Washington, DC: U.S. Government Printing Office, 1996. A 650-page book prepared by the Federal Research Division of the Library of Congress under the Country Studies/Area Handbook Program, sponsored by the Department of the Army. Contains extensive index, bibliography, and appendixes.

Hans Wiessmann, *From Horror to Hope.* New York: German Information Center, n.d. Text and interviews exploring the present-day relationship among Germany, the Jews, and the nation of Israel.

Pamphlets and Booklets

Published by the Press and Information Office of the Federal Government of Germany:

"Culture"

"Education and Science"

"The Federal States"

"Life in the Community"

"Political System, Constitution, Law"

"Vocational Training in Germany"

Websites and CD-ROMs

http://www.government.de/ Contains extensive information and completely updated statistics on all aspects of life in Germany today.

Compact Disc: The Software World Atlas. Novato, CA: Software Toolworks, 1994. Extensive graphs, charts, maps, and lists of statistics on dozens of world countries.

INDEX

Picture Credits

About the Author

Eleanor H. Ayer is the author of more than fifty books for children and young adults. She has written extensively on Germany, Hitlerism, and the Holocaust, including such titles as *Parallel Journeys, The United States Holocaust Memorial Museum*, and several volumes in a series titled *The Holocaust*. In addition, she has written travel guides, books on teenage social issues, and many biographies.

Ms. Ayer has a master's degree in literacy journalism from Syracuse University's Newhouse School of Journalism. She lives with her husband and two sons in a small town north of Denver, Colorado.